The Mughals

The Kings, The Queens and The Begums

The M… als

The Kings, The Queens a… …he Begums

Dr Narayan Raj
and
Syed Rafiuddin Qadri

KALPAZ

ISBN: 978-93-5128-247-1

Price: ₹ 540

First Published, 2017

Published by

Kalpaz Publications
C-30, Satyawati Nagar,
Delhi – 110052
E-mail: kalpaz@hotmail.com
Ph.: 9212142040

Printed at: G. Print Process, Delhi

Cataloging in Publication Data—DK
Courtesy: D.K. Agencies (P) Ltd. <docinfo@dkagencies.com>

Nārā'in Rāj, author.
The Mughals the kings, the queens and the begums / by Dr Narayan Raj and Syed Rafiuddin Qadri.
pages cm
Includes bibliographical references.
ISBN 9789351282471

1. Mogul Empire—Kings and rulers—Biography. 2. Queens—Mogul Empire—Biography. 3. Mogul Empire—History. 4. India—History—1526-1765. I. Qadri, Sayyid Rafi'uddìn, author. II. Title.

DS461.9.A1N37 2017 DDC 954.0250922 23

Dedicated to:

Dr Sheela Raj
A Historian
and
A Scholar of Repute

Contents

Preface

It is a fact that the wealth of India was the wonder and envy to other nations of the World. The natural habitat of India, temperate climate resulting in reduction of human wants and abstemious habits of the people resulted in the increase in natural income of India throughout the sixteenth and seventeenth centuries.

The frequent civil disputes among the princes and the nobles, rebellions against the government was the another cause of insecurity among the people which had serious consequences on the stability and economy of India. There was no foresightedness left among the rulers and leaders. There was no ruler and leader left in the true sense to take forward the new philosophy of life. The throne was left with full of puppets. The frequent civil conflicts, spread a sense of insecurity among the masses. The peasants withheld the land revenue. As a result, the government seized and anarchy commenced.

Unfortunately, the wealth was not used for progressive purpose, such as, development of education, agriculture etc. It was mostly used for efficient national defence. Thus, the wealth only made rulers weak and fatal and tempted the foreign invaders.

Sher Shah once said, "Indians should be made friends as they are useful, when we need them". Humayun made India his house and died in India. Akbar represented these views. Jahangir, Shah Jahan and Aurangzeb married Hindu ladies. If from parental side they were the decendants of Taimur, then from maternal side, they were the children of descent Rajputs.

The decline of the Mughal Empire was mainly due to the inefficiency of the later Mughals to select right Nobles and Wazirs, get work done and develop their talent.

The liberal Akbar, the self indulgent Jahangir and the cultured Shah Jahan had welcomed Shias whereas Aurangzeb did not. The Hindus were not loyal to the later Mughals and turned enemies. The subsequent rulers of Delhi in the eighteenth century were helpless and depended on others. They left the entire administration in the hands of Wazirs. This resulted in intrigues and factions envy against others.

The Mughal Emperors were only their pay masters. The later Mughals were divided into Turani (Central India) and Hindustani parties, both Muslim and Hindu Rajas were with the latter. The division was between Irani (Persian) and Turani (Sunnis). This happened during the second half of the eighteenth century.

The outstanding feature of the Eastern Historians and writers is that they wrote about wars in detail and narrated them nicely. However, the writer of 'Humayun Nama' is a lady who hates wars and their narrations. Therefore, the outstanding feature of 'Humayun Nama' is that it describes only the personal life, economic activities, cultural aspects and the political events. These events clearly indicate the economic activities of that period.

While writing the history of the Mughals, the social, cultural and economic aspects have not been highlighted, only political aspects have been given prominence. The social, cultural and economic aspects have been mentioned in bits and pieces by the writers of Mughal history.

It is, therefore, essential that the Mughal history should now be written in the modern style of 'annales' in which all aspects of the society political, social, cultural and economic have to be written and their inter-dependence on each other brought out to give true picture of life.

While writing the history of the Mughals, the European historians and writers were not fair in their assessment and distorted the facts to a greater extent. They did not project the positive aspects of the Mughal Emperors in detail.

Bahadur Shah 'Zafar', the last ruler, played an important role in maintaining the communal harmony. He was a poet himself and contributed to the development of Urdu literature. He maintained Hindu-Muslim unity and celebrated the festivals of both the communities in his palace.

The struggle for survival did not last long. Bahadur Shah, the last Mughal Emperor was imprisoned by the selfish British and sent to Rangoon, where he passed away.

India witnessed a change with the arrival of the Mughals. These changes can be seen in artistic monuments, cuisines, the work in gold and silver wares that is usually called *zari, zardari* and *chickenkari.* The famous *kim-khwab* brocade and many others.

The fact cannot be ignored that the Begums of the Mughal dynasty were remarkable in many ways. They were beautiful, educated, talented and contributed in socio-economic fields. They were poetesses of repute. Some of them played important roles in politics as well. Their generosity was legendary.

The Queens and the Begums spent most of their personal money in education, establishment of educational institutions, charity, celebrating marriages of the poor girls. They patronised the scholars, poets, who were specially the girls.

Some of the Queens and the Begums had their own libraries. They not only patronised education but also encouraged it among the, girls. They constructed many Masjids, and Madrassas and Travellers' Bungalows.

The Queens and the Begums were ladies of taste and chaste. They were very fond of perfumes. Some of them invented perfumes or '*Itr*'. Nur Jahan's mother, Asmat Banu Begum, prepared an '*Itr*' from rose petals and named it '*Itr Jahangiri*'.

'*Pandan*' was the grace and elegance of the palace. These Begums were very fond of eating '*pan*' i.e. betel leaves with lime, katachue, *supari*, cloves and *iliachi* etc. *Nagardan*, *Ughaldan* would always accompany the *pandan*. They were all made of gold or silver or gold and silver the combination of which is called *Ganga-Jamuni.*

A write up on the Queens and the Begums would be incomplete without mentioning the jewels they wore. They were fond of wearing crown made of valuable jewels and other costly head jewellery, such as, *Sis-phul* later called as *Sis-phul Adharchand, Kotbildar, Bindali, Mang, Mirza Be Parwa* or *Jhumer, Baina Bindya. Baina* are made of gold studded with diamonds, precious stones and pearls. The ornaments of the ear were *Bauli* and *Kundala, Kuntila, Karan Phul, Magrela, Ear Rings* and *Jhumka* etc. The ornaments of the Nose were *Besar, Phuli, Laung, Nath.*

Besides these, the ornaments of the neck, ear and nose need special mention. They were also fond of wearing rings of beautiful designs in their fingers with precious diamonds and sapphires. The Begums used to wear waist belts, ankle and foot ornaments.

The jewellery of the neck, such as, *chintak* made of gold and studded with valuable diamonds and other precious stones etc, *chandan har, pan har, baddhi, pachladi, mala* made of gold. *A satlada* is made of pearls, necklace and *har* made of gold and precious diamonds. The jewellery of the forearms, such as *kada, bazu bandh, kangan, tad* etc. are made of gold studded with diamonds and precious stones. The jewellery of the wrist are of different types made in the form of golden bangles studded with diamonds and precious stones. A ring with round mirror known as '*Aarsi*' with pearls around it was the ring of the thumb of the Begums. The ornaments of the ankle and foot are *durdhani, bichhawar, anwat-nayya.*

It is said that if there is no light, the diamonds of the jewellery of the Begums are sufficient for its replacement.

Besides these, the Queens and the Begums were very fond of wearing beautiful costumes. The Begums wore tight dresses with veil covering their heads. They would cover their body till ankle. The most famous dress being *pishwaz* and *pyjama*.

The garment made of fine muslins, silk, velvets and brocade. The famous *Dhaka Malmal* was common among the muslins. Besides these, satin, *kimkhab, kathan,* tafta etc. were also used.

To design the dresses, laces, *kinari* etc. were used. However, *kinari* was commonly used which was of different types and sizes.

Embroidery of different types was also done. The Kings employed tailors to make clothes for their household.

It is a well known fact that the Mughals had a variety of dishes prepared in their kitchen. They introduced many dishes during their period as they had lovely taste for eating. The Mughlai dishes has a very long list and were famous world over, such as, *Biryani* of different types, the famous mutton *kababs*, mutton dishes of various kinds, chicken prepared in different forms, delicious desserts in different styles.

It is said that the Begums of the palace also supervised cooking in their kitchen even though a large number of chefs were employed for the purpose. Sometimes, they even cooked themselves.

It is a well known fact that Nur Jahan introduced a number of dishes. A finely carved jade and gems studded fruit knife in the Salar Jung Museum in Hyderabad belongs to Nur Jahan is a testimony to this fact. Jahan Ara and Udipuri Begum were also interested in cooking.

The Queens and the Begums of the Royal palace played an important role in maintaining peace and harmony. They acted as mediators in many disputes between brothers. They interfered in the politics of the state and some of them in administration as well.

Chapter - 2

The Kings and The Queens

Sultan Amir Taimur Saheb Kharan

Date of Birth	:	27th *Shaban* 736 AH (9th April 1336 A.D.)
Coronation	:	*Ramazan* 771 AH (April 1370 A.D.) at Qatar Gung.
Ruled for	:	Thirty five years eleven months five days.
Lived for	:	Seventy one years eleven months two days.
Year of Death	:	807 AH (1404 A.D.)
Translation of Chronogram or Chronographic Verses	:	King Taimur, that none was similar to him among the kings was born in year seven hundred and thirty six ascended the throne in the month of Ramazan in the year seven hundred and seventy one. Bid good bye to the world in the year eight hundred and seven Hijri.
Wife	**:**	**Hameeda Banu Begum**

Fig. 2.1: Hameeda Banu Begum, Sultan Amir Taimur Saheb Kharan

Courtesy—Salar Jung Museum, Library Hyderabad, India

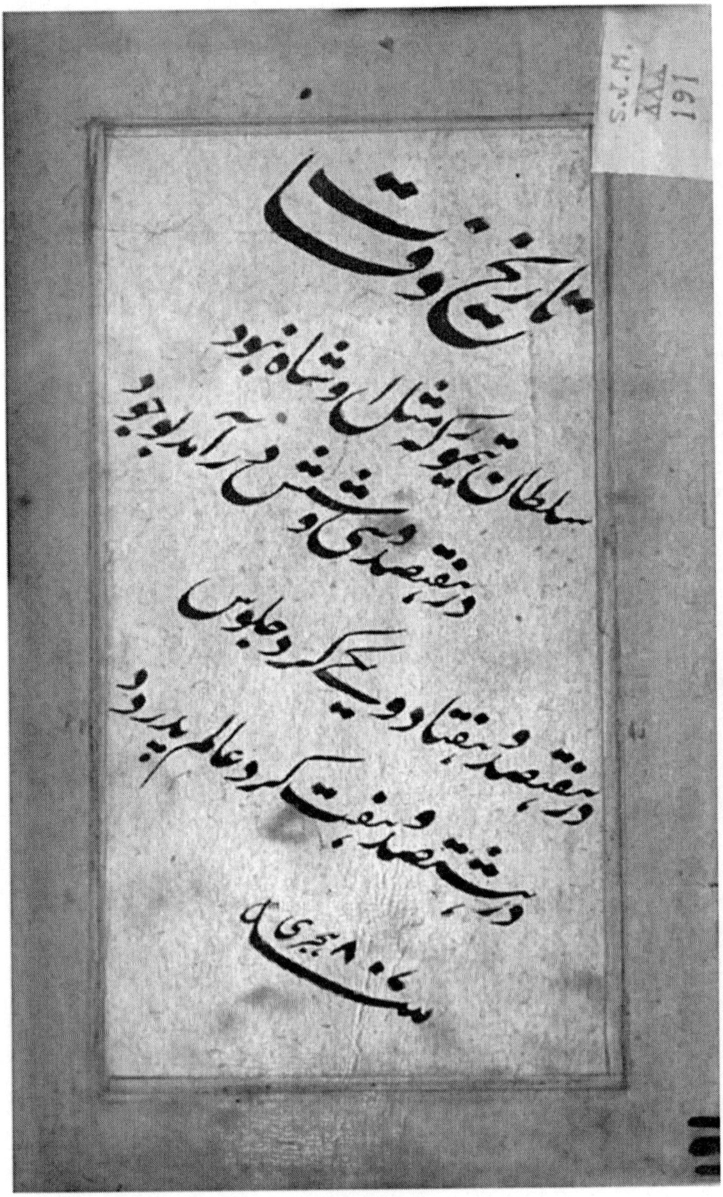

Courtesy—Salar Jung Museum, Library Hyderabad, India.

Fig. 2.2: Chronogram in Persian.

Courtesy—Salar Jung Museum, Library Hyderabad, India.

Fig. 2.3: Gaiti Ara Begum Alias Meher Vish Banu Begum. Jalaluddin Miran Shah.

Jalaluddin Miran Shah

Date of Birth	:	14th *Rabi-us-Sani* 760 AH (14th March 1359 A.D.) Samarkhand.
Coronation	:	17th *Shabanul Moazam* 807 AH outskirts of Iran (Mazafat).
Lived for	:	Forty years ten days.
Ruled for	:	Two years four months ten days.
Year of Death	:	810 AH (1407 A.D.)
Translation of Chronogram or Chronographic Verses	:	King of an era, Miran Shah passed away due to his old age after suffering the grief of old world in 810 *Hijri.*
Wife	**:**	**Gaiti Ara Begum Alias Meher Vish Banu Begum.**

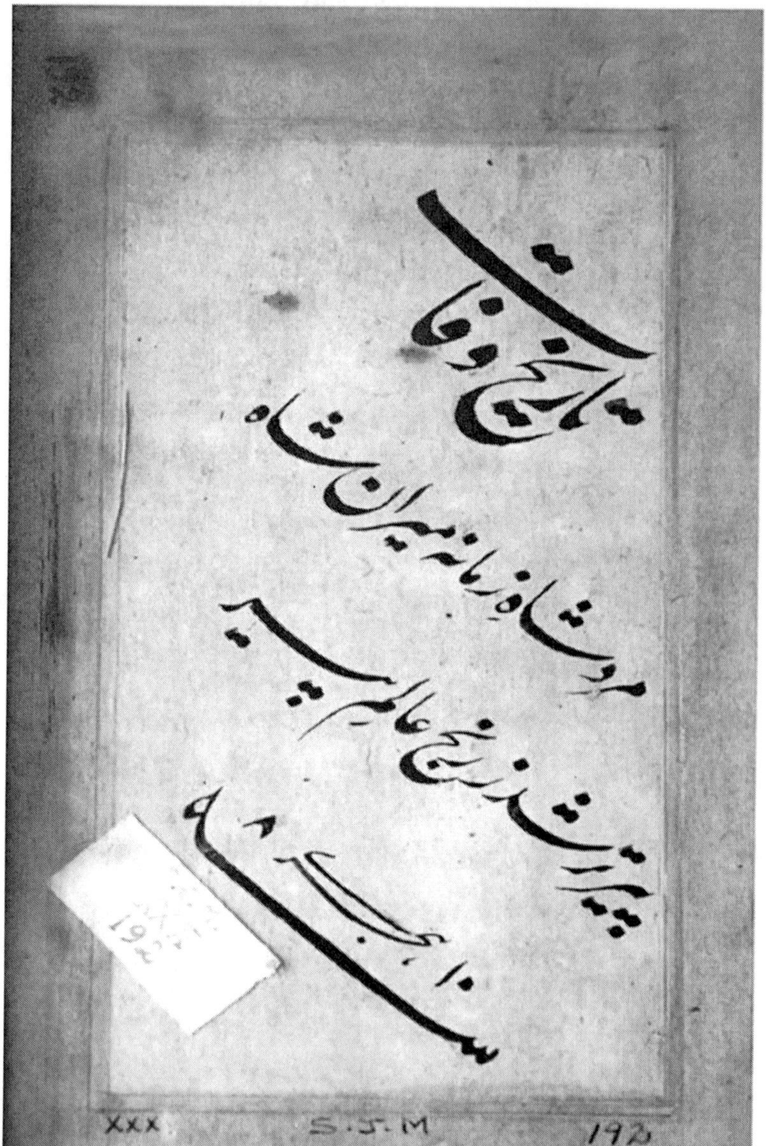

Courtesy—Salar Jung Museum, Library Hyderabad, India.

Fig. 2.4: Chronogram in Persian.

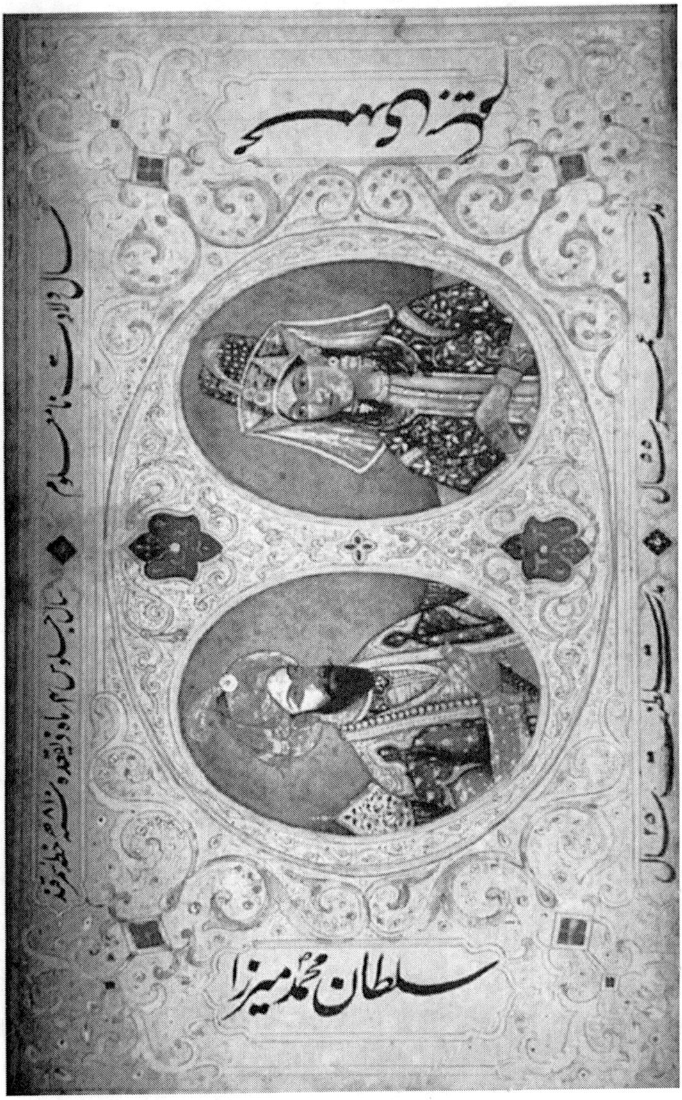

Courtesy—Salar Jung Museum, Library Hyderabad, India.

Fig. 2.5: Sultan Mohammed Mirza Mohammedi Begum.

Sultan Mohammed Mirza

Date of Birth	:	Not known.
Coronation	:	4th *Mahe Ziqhad* 810 AH (28th March 1408 A.D.) at Samarkhand.
Lived for	:	Fifty five years.
Ruled for	:	Twenty five years.
Year of Death	:	855 AH (1451A.D.) at Tabriz.
Translation of Chronogram or Chronographic Verses	:	In the year 855 *Hijri* at Tabriz surrendered soul to Almighty.
Wife	**:**	**Mohammedi Begum**

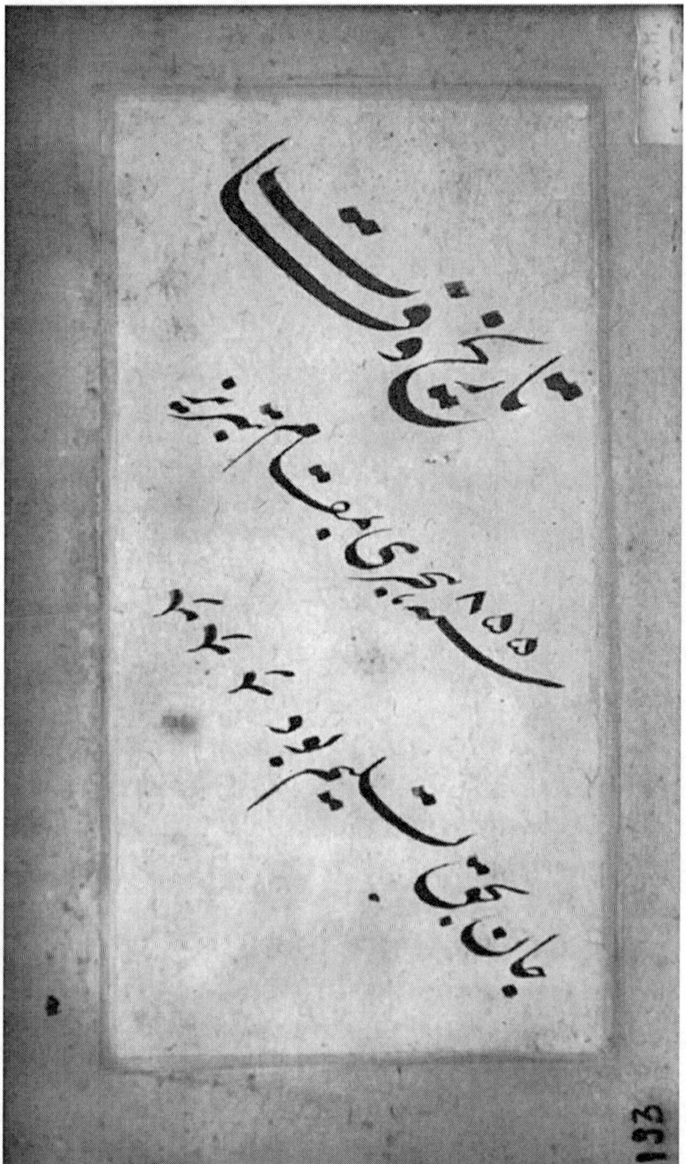

Courtesy—Salar Jung Museum, Library Hyderabad, India.

Fig. 2.6: Chronogram in Persian.

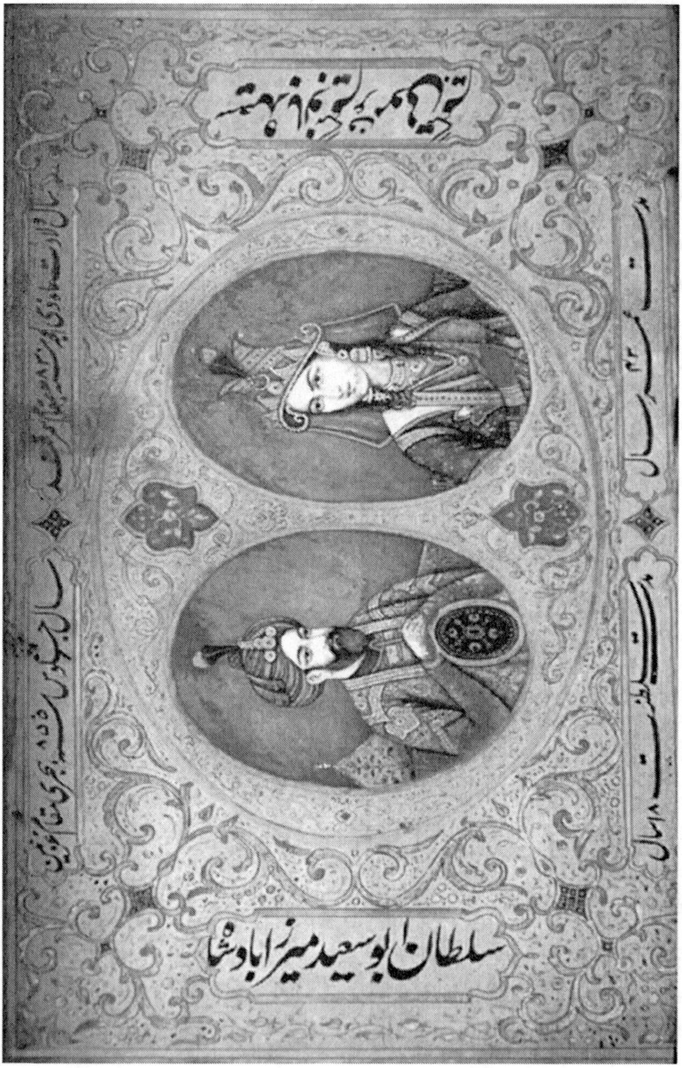

Courtesy—Salar Jung Museum, Library Hyderabad, India.

Fig. 2.7: Sultan Abu Sayeed Mirza Badshah Sayeeda Banu Alias Moti Begum

Sultan Abu Sayeed Mirza Badshah

Date of Birth	:	Month of *Zilhaj* 830 A H (January 1408 A.D.) at Samarkhand.
Coronation	:	855 H (1451 A.D.) at Gaznain.
Lived for	:	Forty three years.
Ruled for	:	Eighteen years.
Date of Death	:	Not known.
Translation of Chronogram or Chronographic Verses	:	Unknown
Wife	**:**	**Sayeeda Banu Alias Moti Begum**

Courtesy—Salar Jung Museum, Library Hyderabad, India.

Fig. 2.8: Chronogram in Persian.

Courtesy—Salar Jung Museum, Library Hyderabad, India.

Fig. 2.9: Qatlakh Nigar Begum   Sultan Omar Shaik Mirza.

Sultan Omar Shaik Mirza

Year of Birth	:	860 AH (1456 A.D.) *ILakha* Samarkhand.
Coronation	:	873 AH (1468 A.D.) at Samarkhand.
Lived for	:	Thirty nine years.
Ruled for	:	Twenty six years.
Date of Death	:	14th *Ramazan-ul-Mubarak* 899 AH (18th June 1494 A.D.)
Translation of Chronogram or Chronographic Verses	:	Due to the demise of Shaikh Omer though lost dignity but taking control of kingdom lies in the power of Almighty. 14th *Ramazan-ul-Mubarak.* Monday 899 Hijri.
Wife	:	**Qatlakh Nigar Begum**

Courtesy—Salar Jung Museum, Library Hyderabad, India.

Fig. 2.10: Chronogram in Persian.

Courtesy—Salar Jung Museum, Library Hyderabad, India.

Fig. 2.11: Zaheer-ud-Din Babar Badshah 'FIRDAUS MAKAN' ***Maham Banu Alias Akter Zamani.***

Zaheer-ud-Din Babar Badshah 'FIRDAUS MAKAN'

Year of Birth	:	6th *Muharram* 888 AH (13th February 1483 A.D.) Kithai (Province) Gharfana.
Coronation	:	At Andajan on 5th *Ramazan*, 899 AH (5th June 1494 A.D.).
Lived for	:	Forty nine years.
Ruled for	:	Thirty seven years eight months one day.
Date of Death	:	6th *Jamadi-ul-Awal* 937 AH (26th December 1530 A.D.).
Translation of Chronogram or Chronographic Verses	:	Epoch making Babar, proficient in justice, endowed with special talent of secrecy of kind creator. The year his soul rests in Paradise, Paradise becomes ever lasting place for King Babar. 6th *Jamadi-ul-Awal* 937 Hijri.
Wife	**:**	**Maham Banu Alias Akter Zamani**

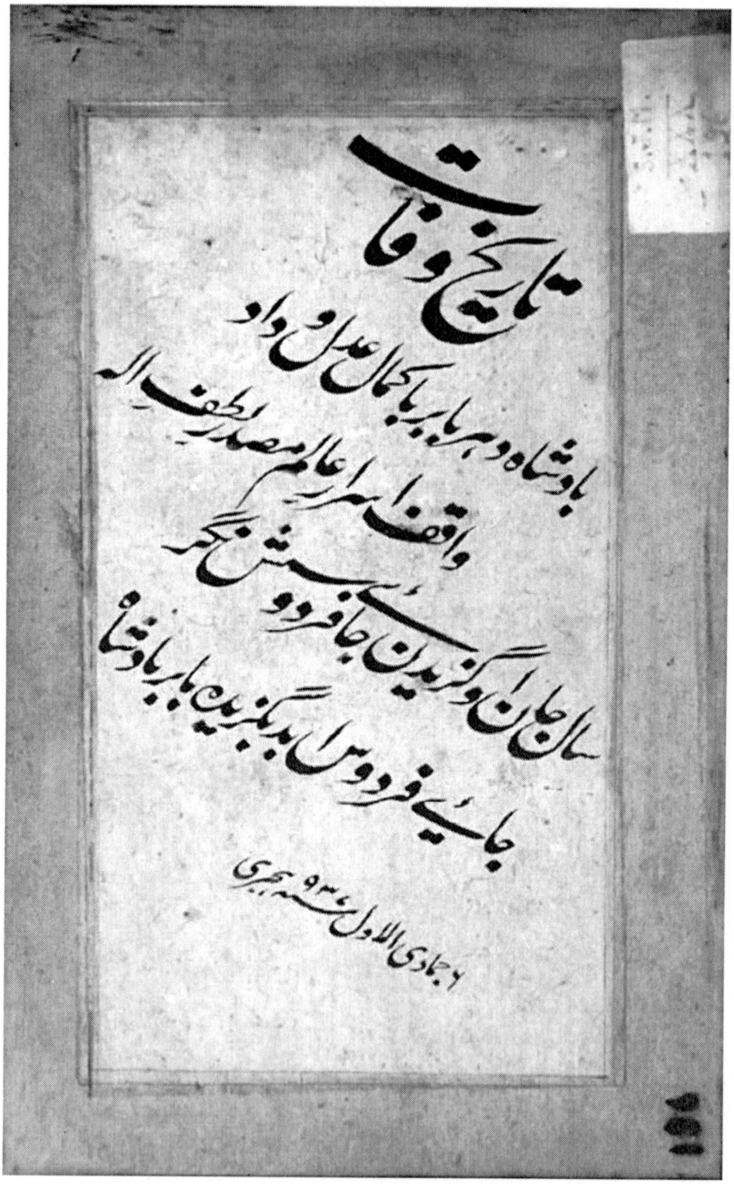

Courtesy—Salar Jung Museum, Library Hyderabad, India.

Fig. 2.12: Chronogram in Persian.

Courtesy—Salar Jung Museum, Library Hyderabad, India.

Fig. 2.13: Hameeda Banu Begum Alias Haji Begum Naseeruddin Humayun Badshah 'JANNAT ASHIYAN'.

Naseeruddin Humayun Badshah
'JANNAT ASHIYAN'

Date of Birth	:	24th *Ziqhad* 893 AH (30th October 1488 A.D.)
Coronation	:	14th *Jamadi-ul-Awal* 937 AH (3rd January 1531A.D.)
Lived for	:	Forty nine years three months twenty six days.
Ruled for	:	Twenty five years two months five days.
Date of Death	:	11th *Rabi-ul-Awal* 960 AH (24th February 1552 A.D.)
Translation of Chronogram or Chronographic Verses	:	Humayun, the king of justice. His special favours for everyone in misery. The date of his death was written as he fell from terrace on 11th *Rabi-ul-Awal* 960 *Hijri.*
Wife	**:**	**Hameeda Banu Begum Alias Haji Begum**

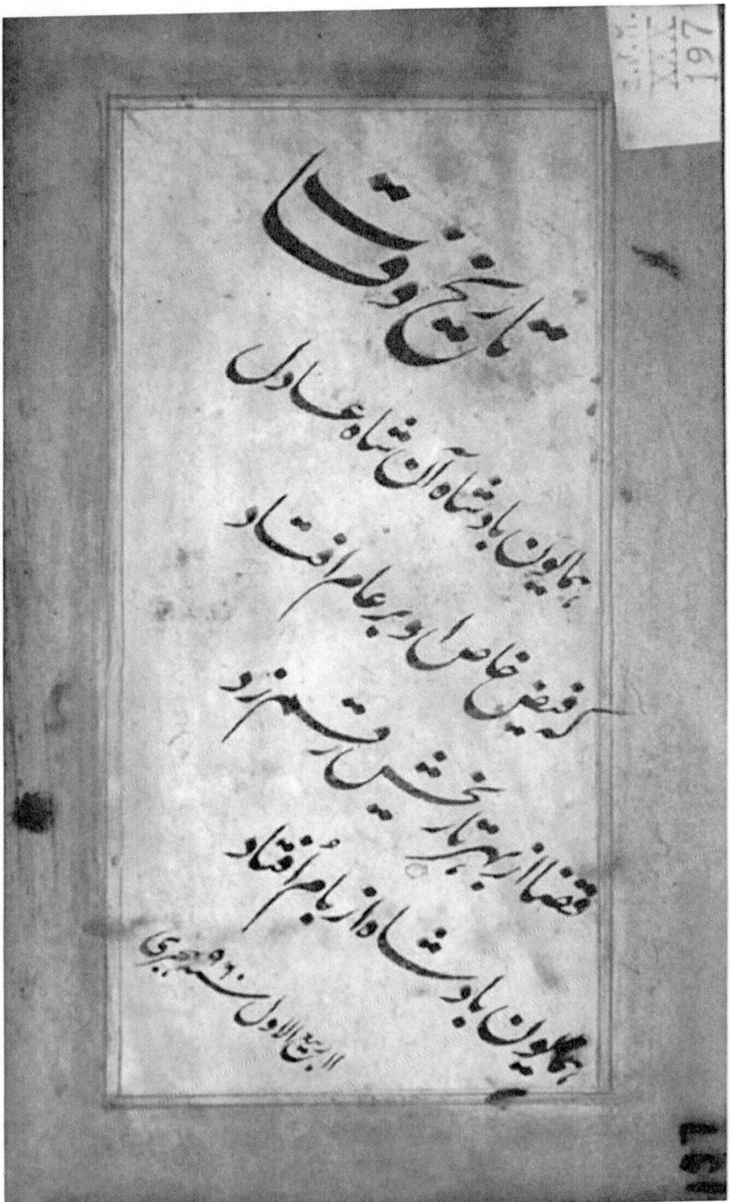

Courtesy—Salar Jung Museum, Library Hyderabad, India.

Fig. 2.14: Chronogram in Persian.

Courtesy—*Salar Jung Museum, Library Hyderabad, India.*

Fig. 2.15: Jodha Bai **Jalaluddin Akbar Shah Badshah 'ARSH ASHIYAN'.**

Jalaluddin Akbar Shah Badshah
'ARSH ASHIYAN'

Date of Birth	:	5th *Rajab* 949 AH (14th October 1542 A.D.) at Amarkot Lahore.
Coronation	:	2nd *Rabi-us-Sani* 963 AH (13th February 1556 A.D.) at Idgah Kalanoor Subha – Lahore.
Lived for	:	Sixty four years eleven months eight days.
Ruled for	:	Fifty one years two months eleven days.
Date of Death	:	13th *Jamadi-us-Sani* 1014 AH (26th October 1605 A.D.)
Translation of Chronogram or Chronographic Verses	:	King Akbar died with the divine call while date composed as "Fout Akbar Shah"/or "Death of King Akbar". 13th Jamadi-us-Sani, Wednesday 1014 Hijri.
Place of death	:	Akbarabad
Wife	**:**	**Jodha Bai**

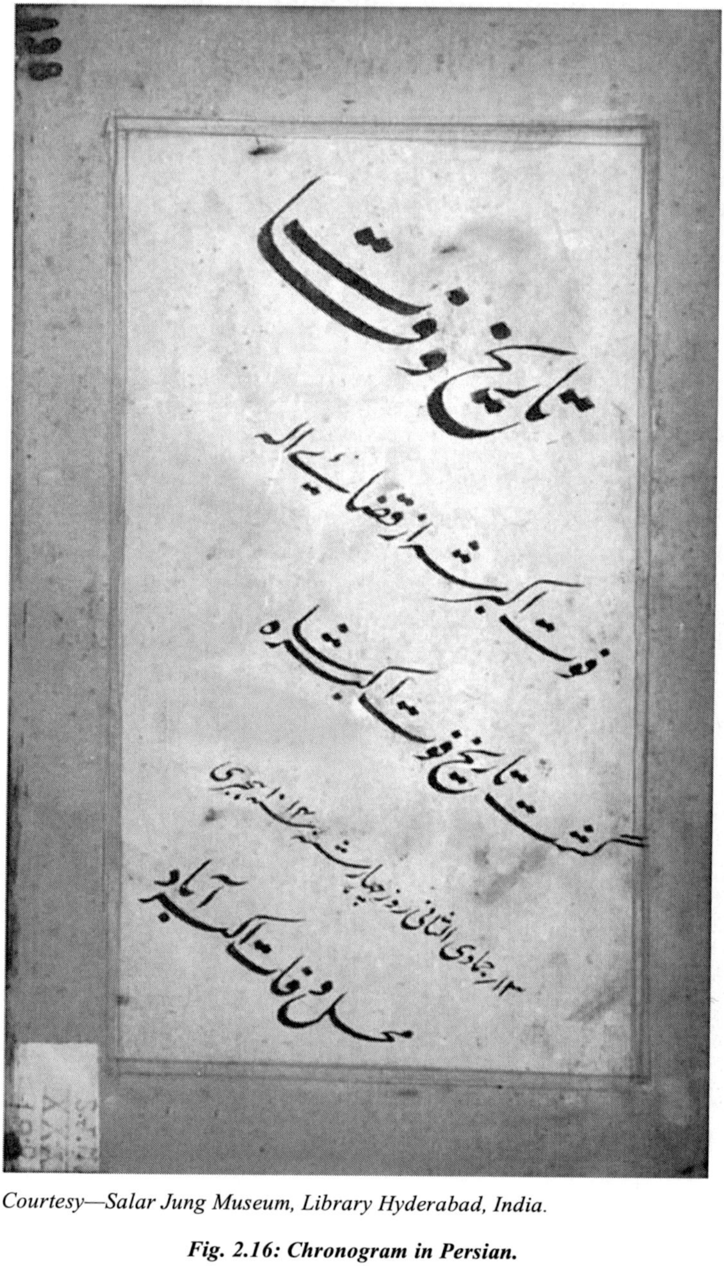

Courtesy—Salar Jung Museum, Library Hyderabad, India.

Fig. 2.16: Chronogram in Persian.

Courtesy—Salar Jung Museum, Library Hyderabad, India.

Fig. 2.17: Nur Jahan Begum

Nuruddin Jahangir Shah Badshah 'JANNAT MAKAN'.

Nuruddin Jahangir Shah Badshah
'JANNAT MAKAN'

Date of Birth	:	1st *Rabi-ul- Awal* 977 AH (13th August 1569 A.D.) at Khasba Fatehpur.
Coronation	:	14th *Jamadi-us-Sani* 1014 AH (27th October 1605 A.D.) at Akbarabad.
Lived for	:	Fifty seven years eleven months seventeen days.
Ruled for	:	Twenty one years eight months fourteen days.
Date of Death	:	27th *Safar* 1036 AH-at Lahore (17th November 1626 A.D.)
Translation of Chronogram or Chronographic Verses	:	Emperor Shah Jahangir his wisdom of justice went to the skies since date of his death came to light 'Ghord' says Jahangir departed from this world. 27th *Safar* 1036 *Hijri*- at Lahore.
Wife	:	**Nur Jahan Begum**

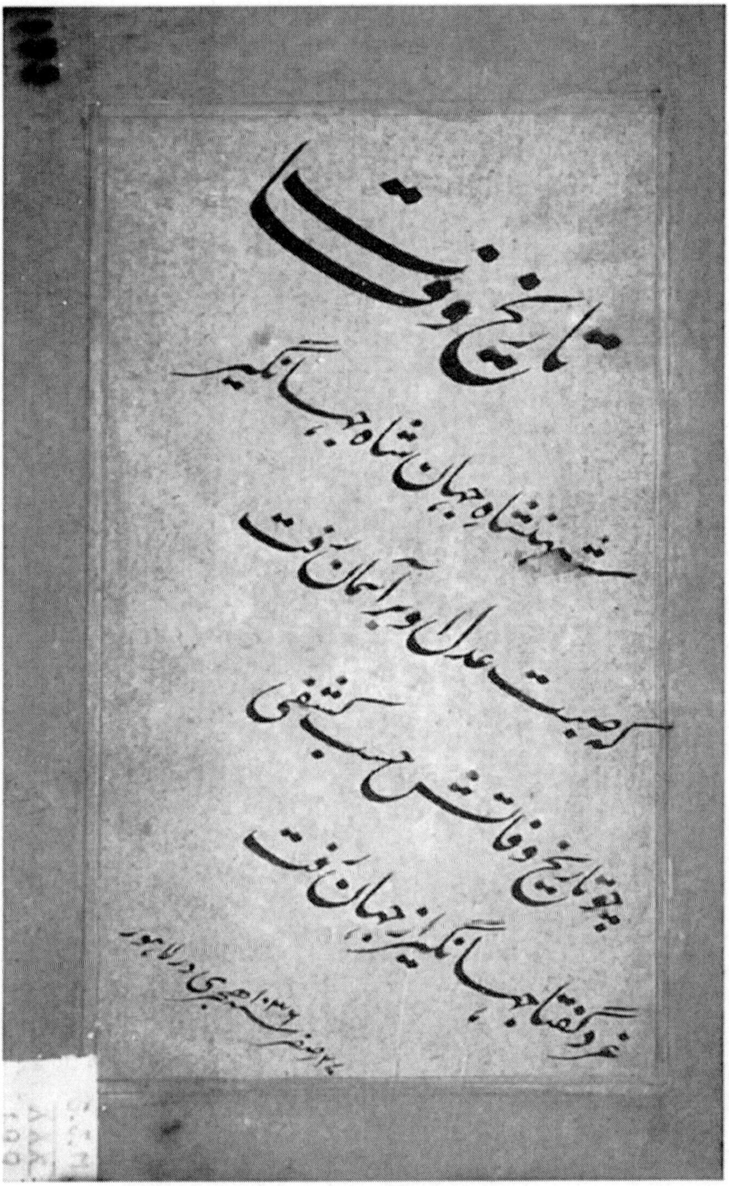

Courtesy—Salar Jung Museum, Library Hyderabad, India.

Fig. 2.18: Chronogram in Persian.

Courtesy—Salar Jung Museum, Library Hyderabad, India.

Fig. 2.19: Shahabuddin Shah Jahan Badshah Mumtaz Mahal. 'AIN MAKAN'

Shahabuddin Shah Jahan Badshah
'AIN MAKAN'

Date of Birth	:	1st *Rabi-ul-Awal* 1000 AH (16th December 1591 A.D.)
Coronation	:	8th *Jamadi-us-Sani* 1037 AH (14th February 1628 A.D.) at Akbarabad.
Lived for	:	Seventy six years four months twenty six days.
Ruled for	:	Thirty one years four months twenty two days.
Date of Death	:	1076 AH (1665 A.D.)
Translation of Chronogram or Chronographic Verses	:	Ashraf Khan composed the year of death of Shah Jahan as "Allah is content with him". 1076 *Hijri.*
Wife	:	**Mumtaz Mahal**

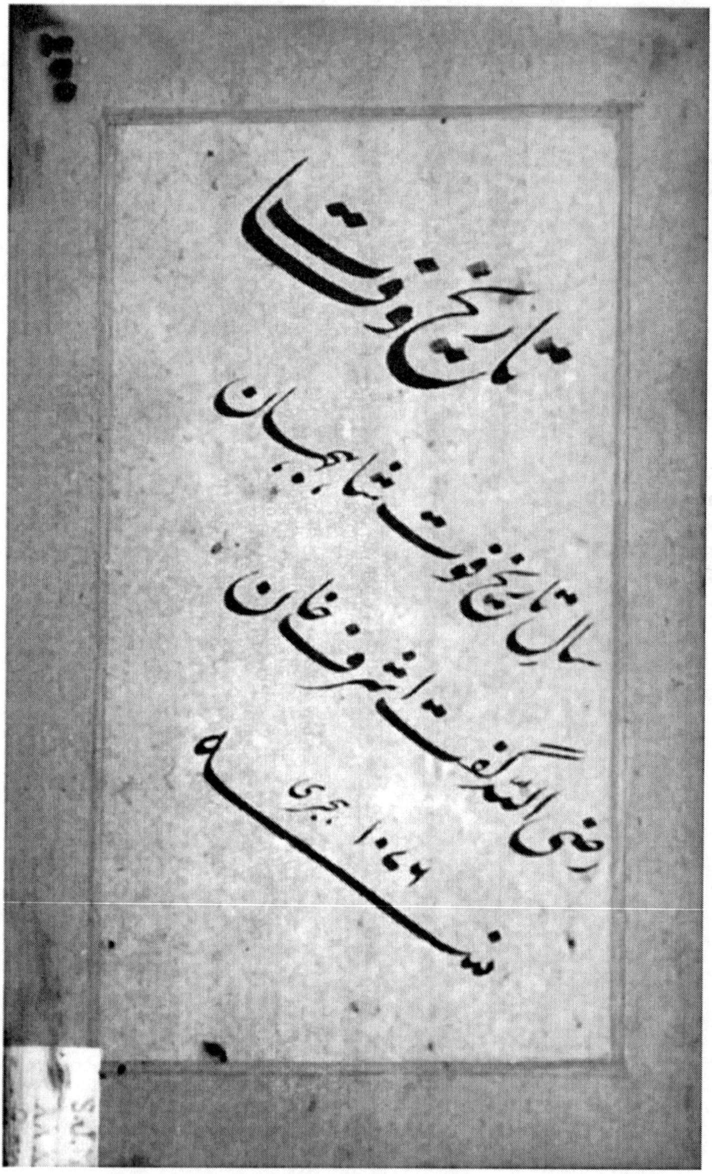

Courtesy—Salar Jung Museum, Library Hyderabad, India.

Fig. 2.20: Chronogram in Persian.

Courtesy—Salar Jung Museum, Library Hyderabad, India.

Fig. 2.21: Maseeh Unisa Begum **Mohiuddin Mohammed Aurangzeb Alamgir Badshah 'KHULD MAKAN'.**

Mohiuddin Mohammed Aurangzeb Alamgir Badshah 'KHULD MAKAN'

Date of Birth	:	11th *Ziqhad* 1028 AH (19th October 1619 A.D.) at Gujarat.
Coronation	:	1st *Ziqhad* 1068 AH (1st August 1658 A.D.)
Lived for	:	Ninety years, fifteen days.
Ruled for	:	Fifty years, twenty days.
Date of Death	:	Saturday 28th *Ziqhad,* 1118 AH (3rd March 1707 A.D.)
Translation of Chronogram or Chronographic Verses	:	Spirit fragrance and Paradise.
Year of Death	:	28th *Ziqhad* 1118 AH
Place of Death	:	Aurangabad
Wife	**:**	**Maseeh Unisa Begum**

Courtesy—Salar Jung Museum, Library Hyderabad, India.

Fig. 2.22: Chronogram in Persian.

Courtesy—Salar Jung Museum, Library Hyderabad, India.

Fig. 2.23: Zeenat Banu Begum Mohammed Muazzam Mulghabib Shah Alam Bahadur Shah-'KHUL'D MANZIL'.

Mohammed Muazzam Mulghabib Shah Alam Bahadur Shah 'KHUL'D MANZIL'

Date of Birth	:	*Rajab* 1053 AH (September 1643 A.D.)
Coronation	:	*Zilhaj* 1118 AH-at Lahore (March 1707 A.D.)
Lived for	:	Seventy years six months.
Ruled for	:	Five years one month.
Date of Death	:	Not Known.
Translation of Chronogram or Chronographic Verses	:	On his death, virtues, bounties, generosity, justice and graciousness have become incoherent ramblings.
Place of Death	:	Mehroli in the vicinity of Delhi
Wifc	**:**	**Zeenat Banu Begum**

Courtesy—Salar Jung Museum, Library Hyderabad, India.

Fig. 2.24: Chronogram in Persian.

Courtesy—Salar Jung Museum, Library Hyderabad, India.

Fig. 2.25: *Jalaluddin Mohammed Farrukh-Siyar Badshah–'SHAHID–I-MARHUM'.* ***Gayti Ara Begum.***

Jalaluddin Mohammed Farrukh Siyar Badshah 'SHAHID–I-MARHUM'

Date of Birth	:	15th *Rajab* 1095 AH (27th June 1684 A.D.)
Coronation	:	23rd *Ziqhad* 1124 AH (22nd September 1712 A.D.)
Lived for	:	Thirty one years eight months twenty days.
Ruled for	:	Six years three months eleven days.
Date of Death	:	8th *Rabi-us-Sani* 1121 AH* (10th June 1709 A.D.)
Translation of Chronogram or Chronographic Verses	:	"Draw a lesson those who have eyes" (This is an Ayat - a verse No. 2 from Surah Hashar under the chapter 22 of Holy Quran). 8th *Rabi-us-Sani* 1121 *Hijri**. His tomb within mausoleum of Humayun Delhi.
Wife	:	**Gayti Ara Begum**

*** The year appears to be incorrect.**

Courtesy—Salar Jung Museum, Library Hyderabad, India.

Fig. 2.26: Chronogram in Persian.

Courtesy—Salar Jung Museum, Library Hyderabad, India.

Fig. 2.27: Rafi-ud-Darjat Mohammed Abul Barkat Badshah **Khujasta Sultana Begum.**

Rafi-ud-Darjat Mohammed Abul Barkat Badshah

Date of Birth	:	7th *Jammad-ul-Akerl* 1111 AH (29th November 1699 A.D.)
Coronation	:	9th *Jamadi-us-Sani* 1131 AH (28th April 1719 A.D.)
Lived for	:	Twenty years one month thirteen days.
Ruled for	:	Three months eleven days.
Date of Death	:	20th *Rajab* 1131 AH (9th June 1719 A.D.)
Translation of Chronogram or Chronographic Verses	:	When the soul of global Emperor of Highest grade leaped under the (blessings of) saplings of forgiveness, Rizwan (in charge) at the entrance of Paradise welcomed and said "Remain here, this is Your abode".
Year of Death	:	Tuesday 20th *Rajabal Marrajjab* 1131 Hijri.
Wife	**:**	**Khujasta Sultana Begum**

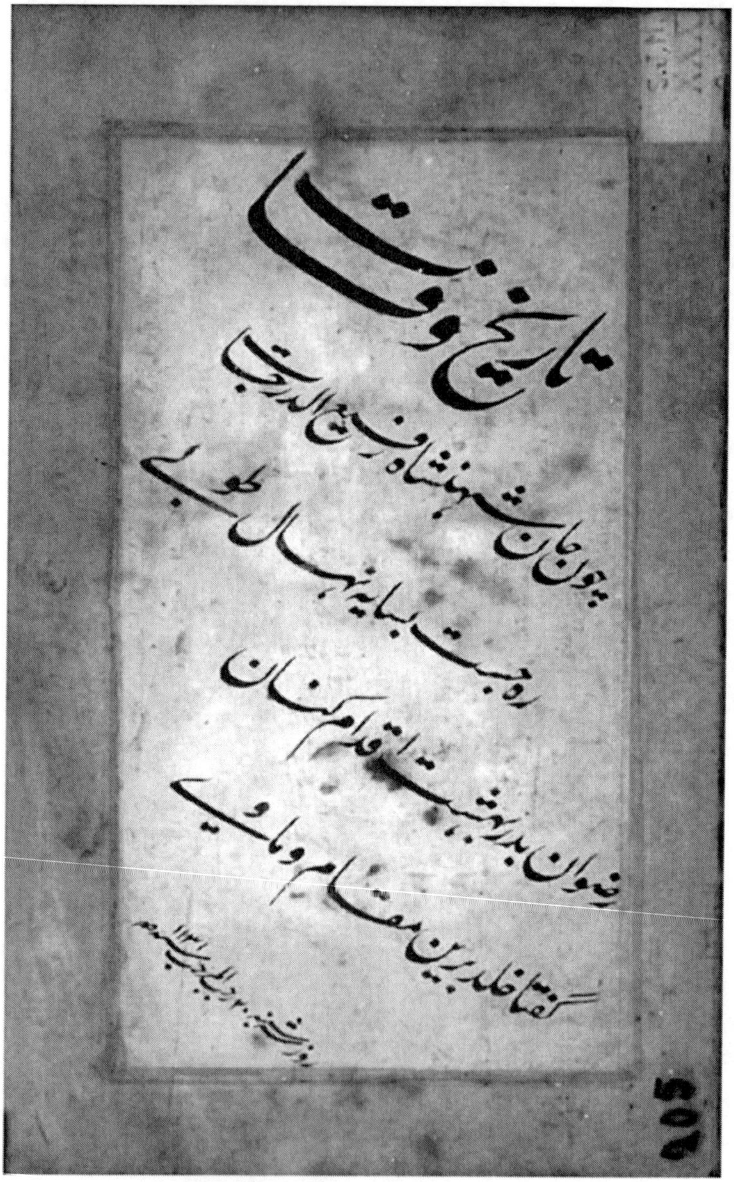

Courtesy—Salar Jung Museum, Library Hyderabad, India.

Fig. 2.28: Chronogram in Persian.

Courtesy—Salar Jung Museum, Library Hyderabad, India.

Fig. 2.29: Sir Hindi Begum Shamusuddin Rafi-ud-Daula Badshah.

Shamusuddin Rafi-ud-Daula Badshah

Date of Birth	:	5th *Safar* 1113 AH (11th July 1701 A.D.)
Coronation	:	20th *Rajab* 1131 AH (7th June 1719 A.D.)
Ruled for	:	Three months twenty seven days.
Lived for	:	Twenty eight years nine months twelve days.
Date of Death	:	17th *Ziqhad* 1131 AH (1st October 1719 A.D.)
Translation of Chronogram or Chronographic Verses	:	Earth has become the abode of Rafi-ud-Daula. His year of death as "Royal Depravities". 17th *Ziqhad* 1131 *Hijri,* buried in graveyard complex of tomb of Humayun–Delhi.
Wife	**:**	**Sir Hindi Begum**

Courtesy—Salar Jung Museum, Library Hyderabad, India.

Fig. 2.30: Chronogram in Persian.

Courtesy—Salar Jung Museum, Library Hyderabad, India.

Fig. 2.31: *Abul Fateh Mohammed Shah Badshah 'FIRDAUS ARAMGAH'* *Shah Rukh Banu Begum*.

Abul Fateh Mohammed Shah Badshah 'FIRDAUS ARAMGAH'

Date of Birth	:	26th *Jamadi-ul-Awal* 1104 AH (5th December 1692 A.D.)
Coronation	:	13th *Muharram-ul-Haram* 1133 AH (13th November 1720 A.D.)
Ruled for	:	Nine years six months one day.
Lived for	:	Forty seven years one month one day.
Date of Death	:	
Translation of Chronogram or Chronographic Verses	:	King of skies, welcomed him abode while sun weathered its brightness (like solar eclipse). When he proceeded (left) towards Paradise from the earth which was like a guest house for five days. A mysterious religious hymn (voice) said "he went to Paradise".
Wife	**:**	**Shah Rukh Banu Begum**

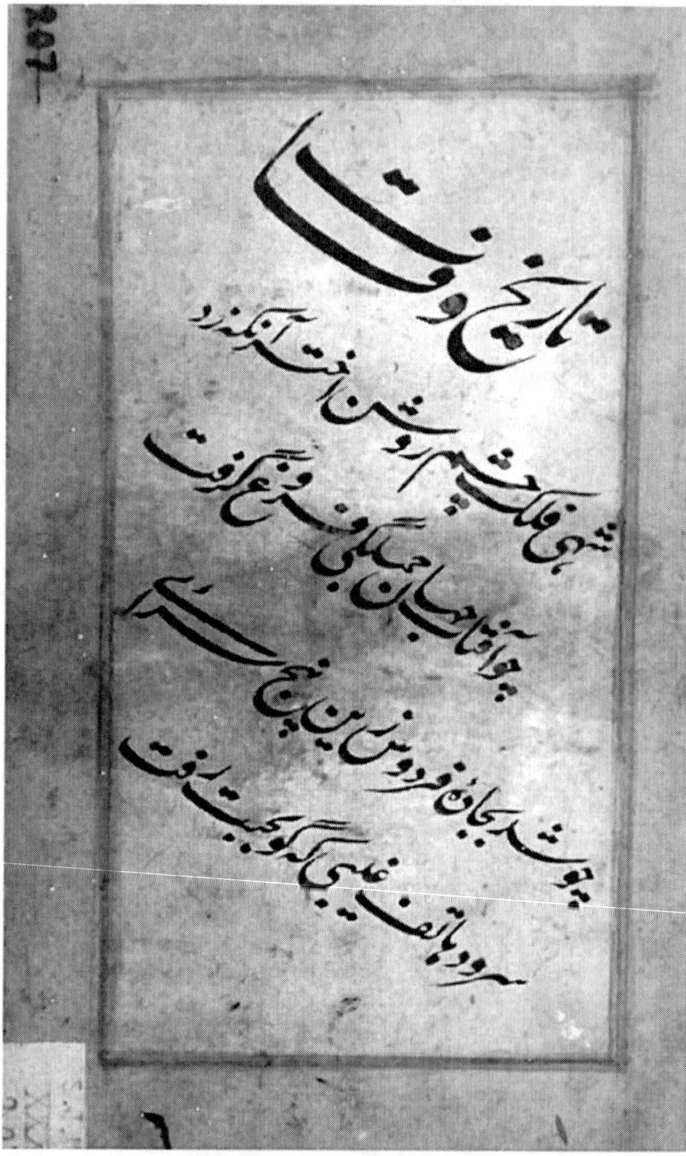

Courtesy—Salar Jung Museum, Library Hyderabad, India.

Fig. 2.32: Chronogram in Persian.

Courtesy—Salar Jung Muszum, Library Hyderabad, India.

Fig. 2.33: Shireen Ligua Alias Aram Jan   Mohammed Moiz-ud-Din Jahandar Shahrah Badshah- 'KHULD ARAMGAH'.

Mohammed Moiz-ud-Din Jahandar Shahrah Badshah 'KHULD ARAMGAH'

Date of Birth	:	10th *Ramazan-ul-Mubarak* 1072 AH (29th April 1662 A.D.) at District of Deccan.
Coronation	:	7th *Muharram* 1144 AH (11th July 1731 A.D.)
Ruled for	:	Ten months three days.
Lived for	:	Fifty two years three months twenty eight days.
Translation of Chronogram or Chronographic Verses	:	By the divine order Farrukh Siyar travelled and became martyr (ed) with the cruelty of the sky. Mysterious hymn (voice) whispered into my ears about this tragic incident. "Alas King Shah Moizuddin died".
Wife	:	**Shireen Ligua Alias Aram Jan**

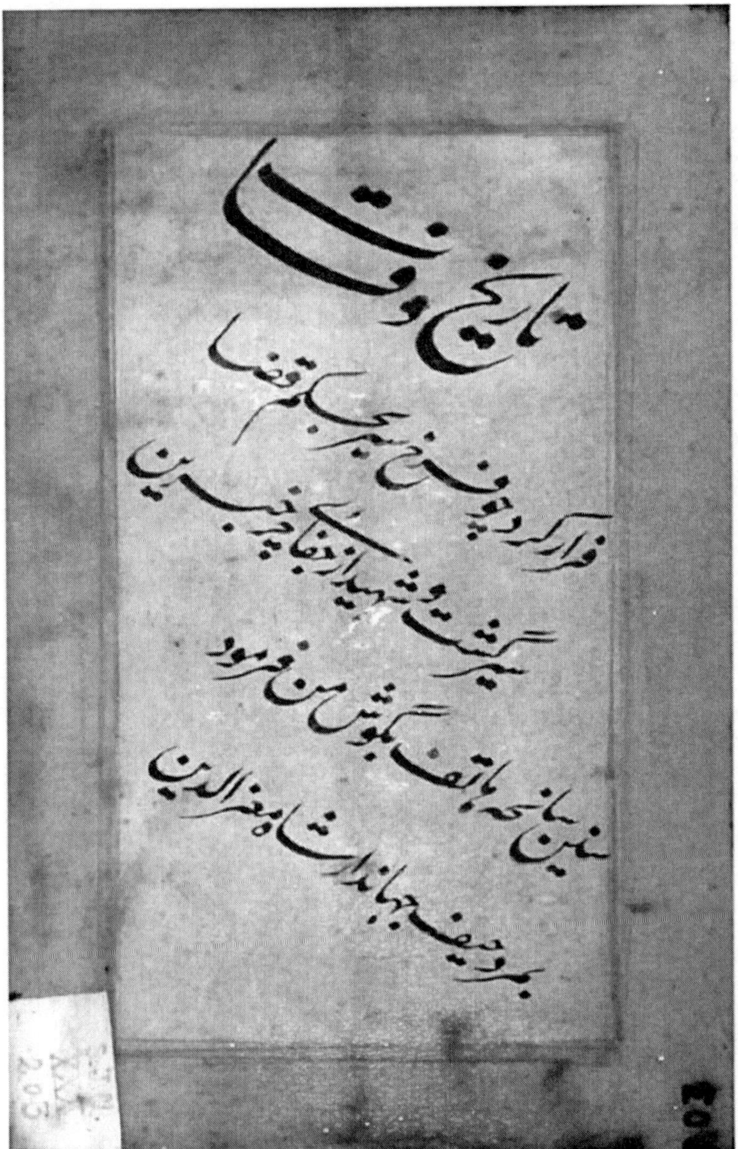

Courtesy—Salar Jung Museum, Library Hyderabad, India.

Fig. 2.34: Chronogram in Persian.

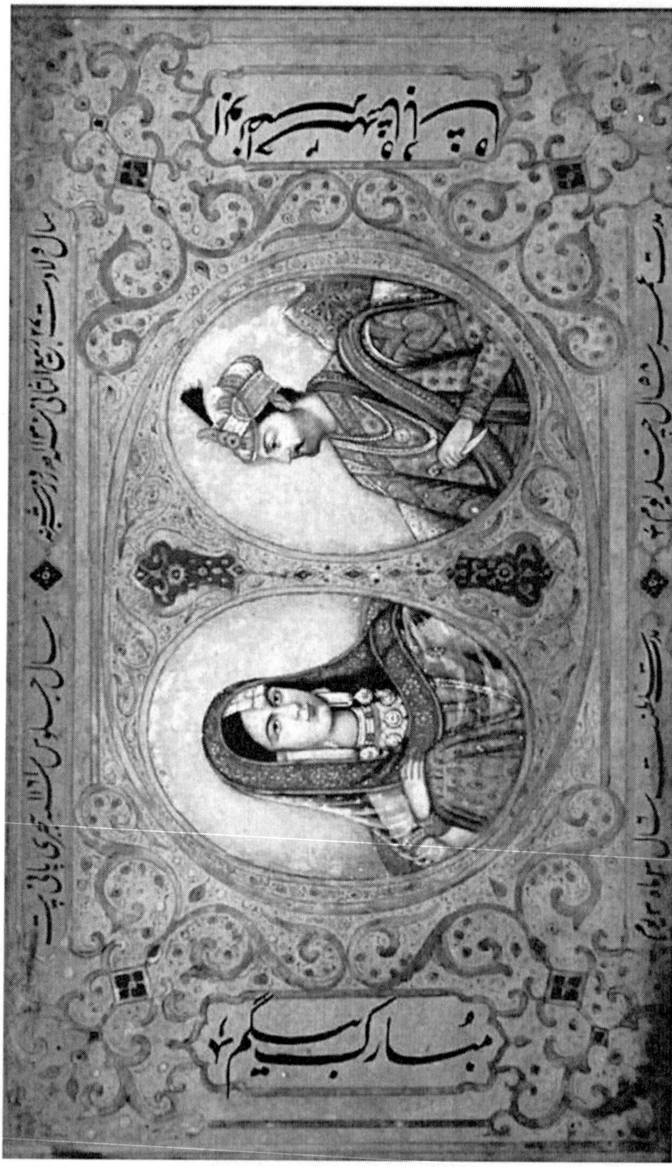

Courtesy—Salar Jung Museum, Library Hyderabad, India.

Fig. 2.35: Mubarak Begum   Abul Naser Ahmed Shah Badshah.

Abul Naser Ahmed Shah Badshah

Date of Birth	:	27th *Rabi-us-Sani* 1130 AH (28th March 1718 A.D.)
Coronation	:	1161 AH (1747 A.D.) at Panipat.
Ruled for	:	Six years three months three days.
Lived for	:	Fifty eight years some days.
Date of Death	:	*1118 AH (1706 A.D.)
Translation of: Chronogram or Chronographic Verses		The Holy warrior packed up his belongings; everyone shed pearl tears from their eye lashes. A mysterious hymn (voice) with a lot of grief composed year of his death "year of his death alas year of his death 1118 *Hijri*". Buried in the outskirts (surroundings) of Delhi.
Wife	:	**Mubarak Begum**

*This date is incorrect.

Courtesy—Salar Jung Museum, Library Hyderabad, India.

Fig. 2.36: Chronogram in Persian.

Courtesy—Salar Jung Museum, Library Hyderabad, India.

Fig. 2.37: *Zubdus-un-Nisa Begum* ***Abul Muzaffar Jalaluddin Shah Alam 'FIRDAUS MANZIL'.***

Abul Muzaffar Jalaluddin Shah Alam 'FIRDAUS MANZIL'

Date of Birth	:	17th *Ziqhad* 1140 AH (12th October 1727 A.D.) at Allahabad.
Coronation	:	4th *Jamadi-ul-Awal* 1172 AH (2nd January 1759 A.D.) at Allahabad.
Lived for	:	Eighty years nine months forty days.
Ruled for	:	Forty eight years four months three days.
Date of Death	:	7th *Ramazan-ul-Mubarak* 1221 AH (18th November 1806 A.D.)
Translation of Chronogram or Chronographic Verses	:	Heavenly Highness King Shah Alam left this mortal world to reside in the Heaven. Year of death of that exalted King is composed with grief "heart strickenly seventh month of fasting (Ramzan)". 7th *Ramazan-ul-Mubarak* 1221 *Hijri-Delhi.*
Wife	**:**	**Zubdus-un-Nisa Begum**

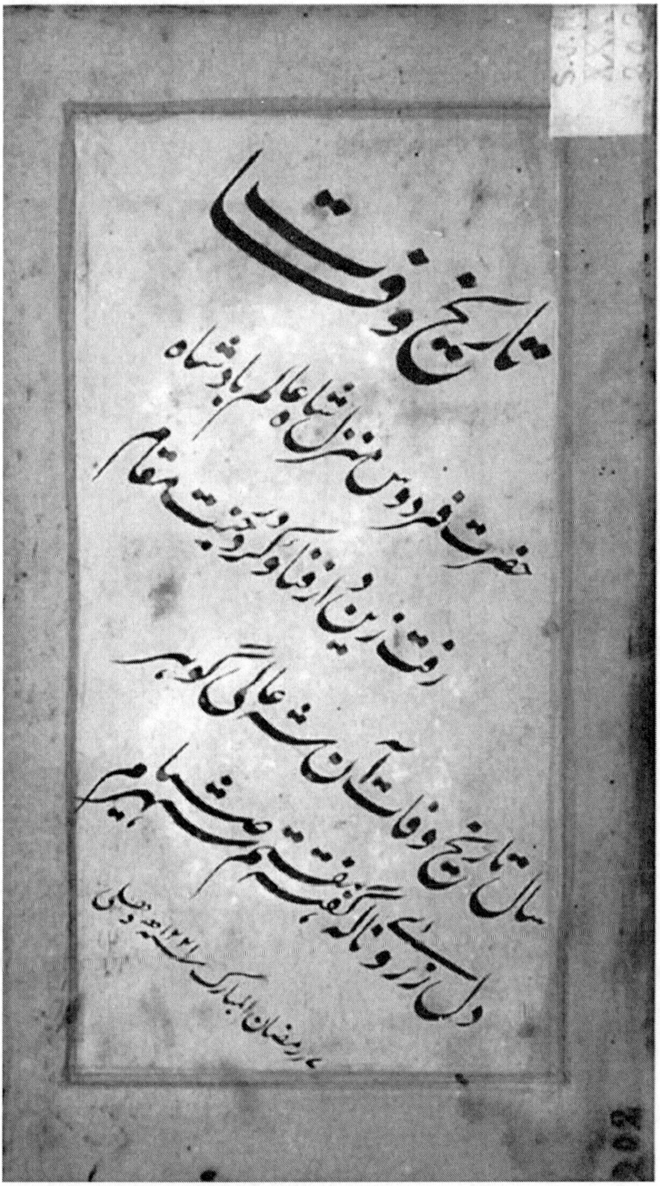

Courtesy—Salar Jung Museum, Library Hyderabad, India.

Fig. 2.38: Chronogram in Persian.

Courtesy—Salar Jung Museum, Library Hyderabad, India.

Fig. 2.39: Mohi-ul-Milat Shah Badshah Akhtar Banu Begum.

Mohi-ul-Milat Shah Badshah

Date of Birth	:	Born in Nau Mahalla Ark Darul-Khilafa-Shahjahanabad.
Coronation	:	1173 AH (1758 A.D.) at Koark.
Lived for	:	Seventy four years few days.
Ruled for	:	One year few days.
Date of Death	:	9th *Safar* 1174 AH (19th September 1760 A.D.)
Translation of Chronogram or Chronographic Verses	:	On 9th *Safar* al Muzaffer 1174 *Hijri* died in Delhi. His tomb is within the mausoleum of King Shah Humayun.
Wife	**:**	**Akhtar Banu Begum**

Courtesy—Salar Jung Museum, Library Hyderabad, India.

Fig. 2.40: Chronogram in Persian.

Courtesy—Salar Jung Museum, Library Hyderabad, India.

Fig. 2.41: Aziz-ud-Din Alamgir Sani Badshah 'ARSH MANZIL'   Lal Kunwar Alias Zeenat Mahal Begum

Aziz-ud-Din Alamgir Sani Badshah 'ARSH MANZIL'

Date of Birth	:	Friday, 1099 AH (1687 A.D.)
Coronation	:	10th *Shaban* 1164 AH. (1753 A.D.)
Lived for	:	Seventy three years few days.
Ruled for	:	Five years seven months twenty seven days
Date of Death	:	8th *Rabi-us-Sani* 1173 AH. (28th November 1759 A.D.)
Translation of Chronogram or Chronographic Verses	:	King Aziz-ud Din hails from Royal ancestors. His place is in the blessings of Allah/Lord. A mysterious hymn (voice) said "he has gone to the Paradise". The honorable judge, the Empyrean King of Seventh sky expressed grief. 8th *Rabi-us-Sani* 1173 *Hijri.* Tomb is within the mausoleum of Humayun-Delhi.
Wife	:	**Lal Kunwar Alias Zeenat Mahal Begum**

Courtesy—Salar Jung Museum, Library Hyderabad, India.

Fig. 2.42: Chronogram in Persian.

Courtesy—Salar Jung Museum, Library Hyderabad, India.

Fig. 2.43: Moinuddin Mohammed Akbar Shah Sani   Kullu Bai Alias Taj Mahal Begum 'ARSH ARAMGAH'

Moinuddin Mohammed Akbar Shah Sani 'ARSH ARAMGAH'

Date of Birth	:	7th *Ramazan-ul-Mubarak*-1173 AH (22nd April 1707 A.D.).
Coronation	:	7th *Ramazan*-1231 AH at Delhi (11th July 1816 A.D.)
Lived for	:	Seventy nine years ten months twenty one days.
Ruled for	:	Thirty one years nine months twenty one days.
Date of Death	:	28th *Jamadi-us-Sani* 1252 AH (9th October 1836 A.D.)
Translation of: Chronogram or Chronographic Verses		The skies blackened by smoke due to sad departure of King Akbar from this world. The foundation of kingdom fell down. His year of death was composed as "Grief of Akbar".
Wife	**:**	**Kullu Bai Alias Taj Mahal Begum**

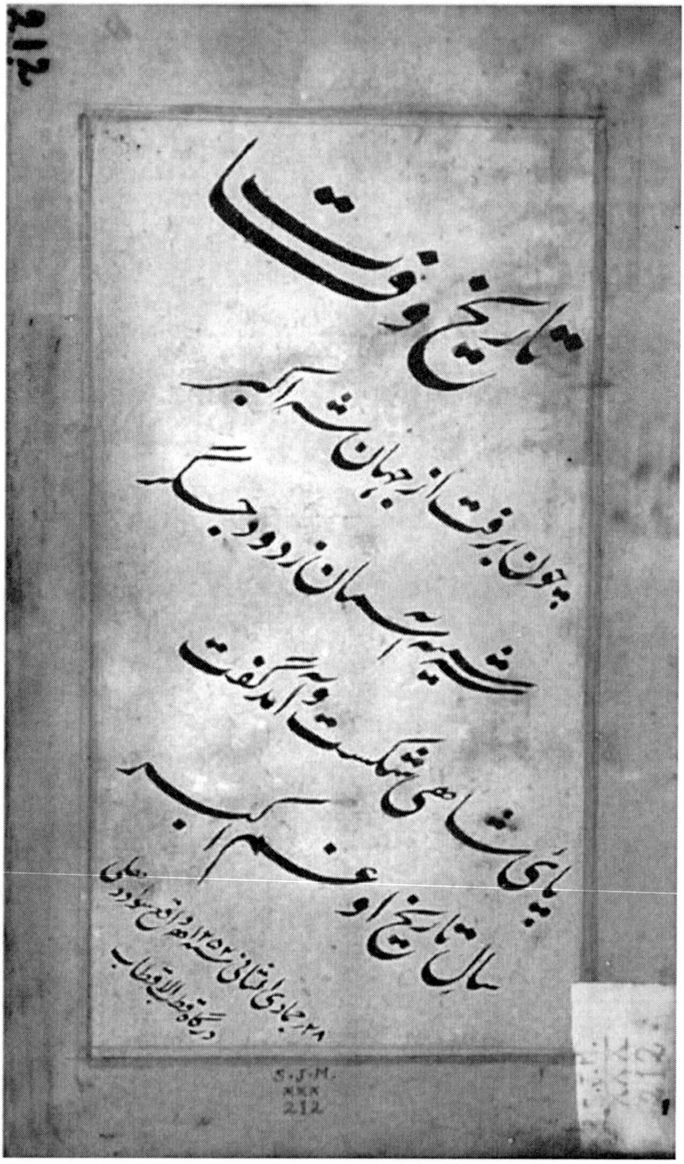

Courtesy—Salar Jung Museum, Library Hyderabad, India.

Fig. 2.44: Chronogram in Persian.

Courtesy—Salar Jung Museum, Library Hyderabad, India.

Fig. 2.45: Zeenat Mahal Begum Abu Zafar Sirajuddin Mohammed Bahadur Shah Badshah.

Abu Zafar Sirajuddin Mohammed Bahadur Shah Badshah

Date of Birth	:	28th *Shaban* 1190 AH (11th October 1776 A.D.) at Delhi.
Coronation	:	28th *Jamadi-us-Sani* 1253 AH (28th September 1837 A.D.)
Lived for	:	Eighty nine years four months two days.
Ruled for	:	Thirty years few months.
Year of Death	:	1279 AH (1862 A.D.)
Translation of Chronogram or Chronographic Verses	:	Sirajuddin Abu Zafar, the traveller went towards Paradise, because of which, the goblet (of wine) was overflowing with joy in Delhi. This is the year of crowning ceremony and now accordingly a mysterious hymn composed the year of his passing away as "Extinguished". Died in 1279 *Hijri* and buried within the precincts of Rangoon (now Yangon in Myanmar).
Wife	:	**Zeenat Mahal Begum**

Courtesy—Salar Jung Museum, Library Hyderabad, India.

Fig. 2.46: Chronogram in Persian.

Courtesy—*Salar Jung Museum, Library Hyderabad, India.*

Fig. 2.47: Mirza Fakhru Valihed (Crown Prince of) Bahadur Shah Badshah Khanum Zamani Begum.

Mirza Fakhru Valihed (Crown Prince of) Bahadur Shah Badshah

Wife : **Khanum Zamani Begum**

Chapter - 3

The Kings

SULTAN AMIR TAIMUR

Taimur came suddenly to India like a storm and looted India and left like a whirlwind. He attacked India several times. Nobody knows the name of his son Miran Shah, grandson Sultan Mohammad Mirza and great grandson Abu Sayeed. Omer Shaik Mirza, son of Abu Sayeed Mirza is famous to some extent.

Taimur's mother was a beautiful lady. Many kings were interested in marrying her. There is a long story about the birth of Taimur. To make a long story short, it must be mentioned that Taimur was born through the rays of Sun. He used to call himself the son of Sun. Thereafter, all the Mughal kings and princes had used Sun on their flags which was the symbol of Mughal Dynasty.

At the time of birth, Taimur had very long hair which were in the shape of crown, because of this, the astrologers predicted that Taimur will rule many kingdoms and the world.

He attacked India several times.

No one can guess his enormous wealth. He paid advance salaries to his soldiers and servants for eight years. He died in the year 1404 A.D. and was buried in Kabul.

Wife:- Hameeda Banu Begum.

JALALUDDIN MIRAN SHAH

After the demise of Taimur, Miran Shah succeeded him. He wanted to become famous like his father. Hence, he always attacked India from different sides but could not conquer it like his father. He only succeeded in plundering and exploitation.

Wife:- Gaiti Ara Begum alias Meher Vish Banu Begum.

SULTAN MOHAMMED MIRZA

He was a staunch Muslim. He was against the idol worship and Hinduism. He attacked Hindus several times and defeated small Rajas. He used to recite 'Quran' several times in a day.

Once, he attacked a Pathan king near the mountain in an open ground and defeated him. During the evening he was passing through thousands of dead bodies. He was very happy and there was no limit to his joy. A Pathan who was hiding among the dead bodies, on seeing the king alone, attacked the king with an arrow and killed him. Thus, the joy and his plans ended.

Wife:- Mohammedi Begum.

SULTAN ABU SAYEED MIRZA

He was a very cruel king and very tough with his subordinates. People decided to kill him. When he came to know that not only his people but the nobles of his darbar had made up their minds to kill him, he took along with him two servants and ran away. His younger brother was coronated. He also ordered the killing of his nobles. The nobles decided to trace Abu Sayeed and made him king. The first thing Abu Sayeed did was to arrest and assassinate his younger brother. This was the only noteworthy contribution of Abu Sayeed.

Wife:- Sayeeda Banu alias Moti Begum.

SULTAN OMER SHAIK MIRZA

He started spreading his empire all over. He was liked by his people. He was fond of pigeon fights.

Not much information regarding his contribution to his social and cultural history is available.

Wife:- Qatlakh Nigar Begum.

ZAHEERUDDIN BABAR BADSHAH 'FIRDAUS MAKAN'

The name Mughal, Turani and Irani will appear frequently in our narratives. The founder of the Mughal dynasty was Babar who was a native of Trans-Oxiana. Turani's were the Sunnis and Iranis were the Shias. Thus, there was a strong feeling of animosity owing to the difference in religion but they used to unite against Hindustanis.

While narrating the views about India, Babar in 'Babar Nama' wrote that India is a vast country in which silver and gold are in plenty. He also wrote in detail about mountains, rivers, animals, flowers, fruits, the dresses, men and women wear, costumes, their way of living in India at that point of time. Babar was a pen man.

When he returned to Kabul from India, he took along with him masons, blacksmiths, carpenters, stone cutters and artisans in large numbers.

The outstanding feature of India is that there were professionals in every field available in large numbers. Thousands of them were available for every work. These professionals were hereditary.

In Zafar Nama, Mulla Sharfuddin Yazde wrote that Amir Taimur constructed a stone mosque for which stone cutters were engaged from India and other countries. Further, when Babar constructed a palace in Agra, six hundred and eighty stone cutters were engaged. Besides this, when he took up construction in Sikri, Bayana, Daultpur-Gwallior and Kabul more than, one thousand stone cutters were working daily for the construction of his palaces. With this, it should be presumed that there were plenty of professionals available for every type of work in India during that period.

People had a lot of affection toward Babar as they saw in him a **man of justice and believed him.**

Wives:- Ayisha Sultan Begum, Zainab Sultan Begum, Maham Begum, Masuma Sultan Begum, Gul-rukh Begum, Dildar Begum, Bibi Mubarika and Mahim Banu alias Aktar Zaman.

Babar was ill for Three months and three days and passed away in 1530 A.D.

NASEERUDDIN HUMAYUN BADSHAH 'JANNAT ASHIYAN'

Humayun was born on 24th *Ziqhad* 893 AH-30th October 1488 A.D. Coronation-14th *Jamadi-ul-Awal* 937 AH-3rd January 1531 A.D. The coronation of Humayun is the addition of a chapter in the history of Taimurians.

When Humayun came to Agra, the decendants of Vikramajit were planning to escape. He organised his soldiers who stopped them. He permitted his admirers to loot and murder them.

They, on their own wished to offer a lot of jewels and presented them to Humayun. Among them was the world famous Diamond '*Kohinoor*' which was brought by Sultan Allauddin. When Babar came, Humayun presented '*Kohinoor*' diamond and thereafter Babar returned it to Humayun.

Humayun as a ruler among the Taimurians and among the Kings and rulers of the world had a distinct position. He was a loving husband, devoted brother, sympathising friend and forgiving father. Maham Begum was the mother of Humayun and the fourth wife of Babar. Humayun's mother Maham Begum passed away in the year 943 AH (1533 A.D). Humayun and Gul Badan Begum were very much saddened and shocked at the demise of their mother.

On the occasion of any celebration, the nobles would present to the king cash and jewellery. When the celebration was completed, as per the orders of the king, it was equally divided into three parts and distributed. One part was kept for the government treasury and distributed among the nobles, ministers and soldiers. The second part called '*Sahadat*' used to be distributed to the scholars, *hakims*, religious scholars, poor and beggars. The third part was called Royal share. The entire portion of cash and jewellery would be presented to the king. The king would order that it should be divided into two parts. One part should be given to the Begums and the other to those present at the ceremony.

It is established from 'Humayun Nama', that women had mastery in music. On the happy occasions, all women of the family would gather at a place and sing. Men also participated in singing but it would be ensured that outsiders were not allowed to join the gathering, specially when women were respected.

Women of that era, besides reading and writing, also had mastery in hunting. After wearing the costumes of men, they used to ride horses.

'Humayun Nama' contains many historical and political events which our history books are devoid of.

When Mahim Begum the wife of Babar came from Kabul, Babar went to receive her. This interesting incident has been narrated in detail by Gul Badan Begum in her own words in 'Humayun Nama'.

No doubt, 'Humayun Nama' contains valuable historical events, it depicts culture, way of living, history, politics etc. It is a valuable document. If any book which can be compared with this is Jahangir's-'Tuzk-e-Jahangiri' and 'Babar Nama' translated by Abdul Rahim Khan Khanan.

It was the earnest desire of Gul Badan Begum that there should be peace among the four brothers of Humayun. They should overcome the differences and live in peace and harmony. It did happen, when there was a armistice between Humayun and Kamran. Humayun organised a big party in honour of his brothers.

Once, Humayun fell seriously ill and there was no chance of his survival. Babar decided to offer his life to save his son Humayun.

As per the old custom, Babar went round the cot of Humayun thrice with a prayer that should Humayun recover, he would sacrifice his life. It so happened that Babar fell ill and was on death bed and there after he died in the year 1530 A.D.

Wives:-Bega (Haji) Begum, Hamida Banu Begum alias Haji Begum, Gunwar-Begum, Shad Bibi, Kanish Agha Khwarizmi and Mah-chuchak Begum.

Humayun selected a place for his burial. The building was under construction. One day Humayun went to inspect it from its top and fell down and passed away. He was buried in this very building.

Humayun lived for forty nine years three months and twenty six days. He ruled for twenty five years two months and five days. He died on 11th *Rabi-ul-Awal* 960 AH-24th February 1552 A.D.

JALALUDDIN AKBAR SHAH BADSHAH 'ARSH ASHIYAN'

Jalaluddin Mohammed Akbar was born on 5th *Rajab* 949 AH (14th October 1542 A.D.).

His coronation took place on 2nd *Rabi-ul-Sani* 963 AH (13th February 1556 A.D.). After his coronation, the foundation of the Mughal Empire was laid for the second time in India.

The decoration and the magnificence of Akbar's *darbar* could be judged from the fact that it has a beautiful octagonal *Ganga-Jamuni* (combination of gold and silver) throne. The throne has valuable and studded with precious jewels, such as, *Almas* (Diamond), Yaqoob (Ruby), *Laal* (red precious stone or red coral) and pearls etc.

He used to perform the *Ziarat* (Pilgrimage) of Khwaja Moinuddin Chishti every year. Sometimes, he used to go from Fatehpur Sikri or Agra to Ajmer on foot.

It was customary during Akbar's period that till the 17th or 18th day of *Nauroz* everyday, the king would be invited to the palace of the nobles and *amirs* and different types of precious jewels, expensive clothes and other items like elephants, horses used to be presented to the king. The king would inspect them and whatever items, he liked, he would take and the rest, leave it to the nobles and *amirs*. Jehangir abolished this tradition.

Akbar constructed many world famous buildings, such as, Bengali Mahal in Fatehpur Sikri, Akbarabad on the banks of River Jamuna,

Humayun's Tomb in 977 AH (1569 A.D.) which took about eighteen years to complete and many others.

He collected valuable literature from various sources in Delhi, such as, books of prose, poetry, in Hindi, Persian, Kashmiri, Arabic.

Every year *Majudat* was conducted. At a fixed time, scholars used to read a book and Akbar used to listen to it. Never a page of a book is left without reading. Once a book was completed, the reader used to be suitably rewarded based on number of pages, he read.

In 980 AH (1572 A.D.) Akbar decided to get the 'History of Ulfi' written. He consulted various scholars. The difficulties faced in writing the Tariq-e-Ulfi was that the historical events of Humayun were not recorded in the form of a book. After a long deliberation, it was decided that this work be entrusted to two persons, one was Johar and the other was Gul Badan Begum, sister of Humayun. Initially Gul Badan Begum was trying to avoid but on the insistence of Akbar, she agreed to write.

Specially, a Department of Translation was set up and a research centre established. Many books were translated from Sanskrit, Arabic, Turkish into Persian. Ramayana and Mahabharata were translated in Persian. Many translators were appointed for this work. Scholars like Gangadhar, Mahesh Anand, Jagdeesh were appointed to help in Sanskrit translation. Some of the noted books published in Akbar's era were History of Ulfi, Ramayana and Mahabharata and titled Ramazan Nama, Tuzuk-e-Babari. It is a translation from Turkish into Persian. (This book was very much appreciated by Akbar), History of Kashmir, Akbar Nama. Lailawati is a mathematics book translated from Sanskrit into Persian.

These books have been written and translated by outstanding authors and translators.

Wives:- Ruqaiya Begum, Salima Sultan Begum, Jodha Bai, the Princesses of Merta and Dungarpur, Bibi Daulat Shad.

Akbar died on 26th October 1605 A.D. and was buried at Sikandra, a place which was selected and got it constructed by Akbar himself.

ABUL MUZZAFAR NURUDDIN JAHANGIR SHAH BADSHAH 'JANNAT MAKAN'

Jahangir was born on 1st *Rabi-ul-Awal* 977 AH (13th August 1569 A.D). He was a good looking person. His coronation was organised on 14th *Jamadi-us-Sani* 1014 AH (27th October 1605 A.D.) at the age of twenty eight years.

It is a fact that India has thousands of castes, different religious sects and ceremonies. Jahangir used to celebrate Dassehra festival along with his nobles. In fact, he described in his own words the Dassehra festival of Agra. The festival of Rakhi was also celebrated by Jahangir. During the reign of Jahangir, Gold and Silver coins were in vogue.

Forceful conversions into Islam from other religions were strictly prohibited. He brought many refinements and reforms in administration, culture, customs and traditions.

Jahangir never hesitated to meet Hindu and Muslim religious personalities or scholars. He never hesitated to listen to their advice.

He performed his weighing ceremony (*Tuladan* ceremony) on the occasion of his eighteenth year of coronation and sent Rupees Two thousand to Shaik Saleem Chishti. He would meet Hindu and Muslim intellectuals and offer them robes of honour.

Once, Rana Amar Singh came to the King along with his two sons and accepted the service and presented a big *Laal* (Red precious stone or a red coral) which was famous in his family, seven elephants and nine horses. Shah Jahan also treated him well by offering Rana robes of honour, a sword studded with precious jewels, *bazubandh* studded with jewels and silver wares for the elephant.

It was customary that Raja and Raj Kumar never used to go together therefore on return he sent Raj Kumar to the Prince. The Prince also offered Raj Kumar the robes of honour and a sword studded with jewels.

Amir Jalaluddin who was the Ambassador of Jahangir at *Adil* Khan Bijapuri, presented a dagger which had a *yaqoob zard* (Red ruby) studded at the handle which was of a very high quality and size of a chicken egg.

Jahangir was very fond of *Itr* (perfume) invented by the mother of Nur Jahan. He was also fond of hunting and music. He had high regards for the poets. He gifted a golden sword to Syeda Jeelani for his Qasida, sometimes he himself wrote ghazals.

Jahangir was interested in the development of public places. He ordered saplings to be planted from Multan to Allahabad alongside the road. The saplings were planted at a distance of one furlong to help travellers to measure the distance they covered.

Wives:- Man Bai, Jodh Bai or Jagat Gosain. He had many more wives but the chief and prominent was Nur Jahan Begum.

He died on 27th *Safar* 1036 AH (17th November 1626 A.D.) at the age of sixty years. He was buried in the garden which was made by Nur Jahan Begum.

SHAHABUDDIN SHAH JAHAN BADSHAH 'AIN MAKAN'

Shah Jahan was born on 1st *Rabi-ul-Awal* 1000 AH (1591 A.D.) Akbar came to see his grandson on Chatti day.

The coronation of Shah Jahan was organised on 8th *Jamadi-ul-Sani* 1037 AH (14th February 1628 A.D.).

After ruling for eleven years from Agra, Mughal Emperor, Shah Jahan, conceived the idea of making Delhi as the new capital. As such, the foundation for the fort at Shahjahanabad -Delhi was laid on 12th *Zil Hijja*, 1048 AH. When the fort was ready, Mukaramat Khan, the supervisor, requested the king to inspect it. The latter came down from Agra to Delhi and entered the magnificent citadel on 24th *Rabi-ul-Awal*, 1057 AH from the door opening towards the Yamuna River side.

Pomp and grandeur marked the convening of the court for the first time in *Diwan-e-Aam*. Following is the account of the Royal entry written by historian, Amad Saleh Kamboh.

The star of the sovereign king is undoubtedly on the ascent. Like the celestial magnificence, the splendor and glory, the power and pelf of Shah Jahan has a permanency to it. The king of the kings took the path of Khwaja Qizar along the river side to enter the fortress. The entire path leading to it was decked up and illuminated for the emperor who is to the terra firma what the sun is to the firmament. The needy and deprived from across the world throng his court to receive aid and succor from his hands that ravel in giving.

Much before the emperor arrived, the royal fort was decorated and the workforce of the kingdom had taken care to embellish and enliven the royal palace and the *Diwan-e-Khas* for the celebration. Colourful carpets made in Kashmir with a touch of elegance and finesse were laid out to the length and breadth of the rooms. The majestic palace with lavish gold and silver ornamentations presented a picture of grace and splendor and signs of ecstasy.

The roof and the walls of the *Diwan-e-Aam* were draped with exceptional and invaluable golden hued fabrics while the chambers and galleries sported embroidered velvety curtains. A large awning measuring 70 yards in length and 45 yards in width manufactured in a factory at Ahmadabad over a long period at a cost of Rupees One Lakh was raised on four silvery pillars to a height of 22 yards. This canopy covered an expanse of 1200 yards and beneath it could easily sit 2000 persons. A three thousand strong workforce was requisitioned to set it up.

Around this canopy were small canopies made of expensive velvet brocade erected on gold and silver columns and covered with silver fencing all around. The royal tent was set up under the big awning on silvery pegs, Irani velvet brocades embellished it while pearl strings dangled everywhere. All over richly adorned golden thrones were laid and amidst them was the regal palace with a golden fencing around it.

On this occasion, the munificence of Shah Jahan came to the fore. In a display of large-heartedness he bestowed rewards and honours. Khadima Begum Jehan Ara was given away Rupees One Lakh while Prince Dara Shikoh was conferred a robe of honour along with arms and his rank was raised to '*das hazari*'. Besides cash of Rupees Two Lakhs and an elephant with caparison was offered.

Prince Sulaiman Shikoh and Sipihr Shikoh, sons of Dara Shikoh were granted pensions of Rupees 500 and Rupees 300 respectively in addition to the salary. Prime Minister, Sadulla Khan was granted a robe of honour, a sword studded with precious stones and rank of '*Saat Hazari*'. Raja Bathal Das was honoured with a robe, '*Panch Hazari*' rank and 4000 strong cavalry. Mukaramat Khan, under whose supervision the fort was built, was honoured with '*panch hazari*' rank.

The people were generally prosperous and happy during his reign. There was a progress in all spheres of life. Industries progressed on a large scale. He was interested in donating large sum of money during famines at various places.

The Peacock Throne (*"Takht-e-Taoos"*) was made during the reign of Shah Jahan in the year 1042 AH (1632 A.D.). It took seven years to complete it under the supervision of Sayeed-e-Gilani alias Behadal Khan Superintendent of Treasury.

Shah Jahan gave jewels weighing 50 Mushkal costing Eightysix Lakh rupees, besides this, he gave One Lakh tolas of Gold costing Rupees fourteen Lakhs. The length of the Peacock Throne was 3.25 yards, the breadth 2.5 yards and height five yards.

Inside the roof, the *Meena* work was done and outside *Laal* (Red precious stone or red coral), ruby, *yaqoob* (ruby) were fixed and twelve pillars were erected and on this two peacocks were made with different types of jewels, between them one tree was made of Laal (Red precious stone and red coral), diamond, *zammarud* (emerald/panna) and pearls. To climb the throne three steps of murassa (different precious stones) were made, around them, there were seven planks of which the middle plank was made of *Laal* (red precious stones or red coral) which was presented by King Abbas Wali of Iran to Jahangir on which the names of Taimur, Mirza Shah Rukh, Mirza Alagh Baig names were carved and Shah Abbas also got his name included in them. Later, Akbar and Jahangir's names were carved. Thereafter, Shah Jahan also added his name.

Mohannad Jan Qudsi wrote a poem during 1055 AH (1645 A.D.) which after the orders of Shah Jahan was engraved on it.

The immense booty including the Peacock Throne that Nadir Shah carried with him did not remain with him for a long period. The Peacock Throne made of Gold, richly jewelled and detachable pillars, steps and roof was stowed away in loose condition. It was to be assembled and placed in the darbar during the coronation ceremony of the king but otherwise it was kept in loose condition.

However, these parts were looted and taken away and dispatched in different quarters. Therefore, the genuine Peacock Throne of Shah Jahan no longer exists in any part of the world. A cheap imitation of it is made by the subsequent kings of Persia. It is still preserved at Tehran-Iran.

Eight years after the invasion of Nadir Shah, he was assassinated and his hoarded treasures were plundered and dispersed.

Shah Jahan constructed world famous buildings, such as, Roza Mumtaz Mahal in 1057 AH (1647 A.D.) at the cost of six crores (60 million), Jamia Masjid in Ajmer in 1047 AH (1637 A.D.), the Shah Jehanabad Fort (Red Fort) in 1050 AH (1640 A.D.), Jama Masjid Delhi 1060 AH (1649 A.D.), Moti Masjid in Agra in 1066 AH (1655 A.D.), Sheesh Mahal, *Diwan-e-Khas, Diwane-e-Aam*, Angoori Bagh, Garden in Kashmir, a Masjid in Dhaulpur in 1046 AH (1632 A.D.), a Masjid in Shaharkutta. He then constructed a beautiful marble building in Kabul.

Wife:—Arjumand Banu Begum, later known as Mumtaz Mahal. Shah Jahan died in 1076 AH (1665 A.D.).

MOHIUDDIN MOHAMMAD AURANGZEB ALAMGIR BADSHAH 'KHULD MAKAN'

Aurangzeb had five sons and five daughters but only three sons were alive during his life time. The second son Muhammed Mauzzam became his heir apparent.

Aurangzeb would write with his own handwriting 'Kalam Majeed' and sell it. The proceeds of this would be utilised for his own expenses. He had not taken any money from the government treasury for his personal expenses. He distributed money for charity with his own hands.

Aurangzeb opened a school 'Dar-ul-Uloom' in every big city in India. The teachers were appointed and their salaries paid from the government treasury. He opened schools for dumb and handicapped and also shelter houses. He organised the purchase of books and made available in every library.

He was a kind hearted person. Those who used to fight against him, Alamgir had respect for them. He was a very strict follower of religion but never interfered in other religions. He neither interfered in Hinduism nor Christianity.

The mother of the heir apparent Prince Muhammed Mauzzam was a Rajput but Alamgir never interfered in her religious matters. She was given full liberty. Inspite of this, the fact cannot be ignored that he destroyed and damaged many Hindu Temples and religious places.

Aurangzeb was a literate person. He knew Arabic and Persian and other Indian languages. He was a good writer and sometimes he had written in poetry as well.

We have narrated good qualities but it would be fair to mention the other side of the picture.

As mentioned above, he destroyed and damaged many temples throughout India and specially, wherever, he went.

He imprisoned his father, Shah Jahan and kept him for several years in prison. As a result, Shah Jahan had to lead a miserable life in prison before his death.

He also imprisoned his own brothers i.e. Dara Shikoh and Murad. Shuja was sent out of India and it is not known where he died.

Arjumand Banu Begum was the mother of Jahan Ara. She advised Shah Jahan and left a 'Will' that her entire personal property and cash be divided in two equal parts, one part be given to Jahan Ara Begum and the other part to be divided into four parts and distributed to four princes i.e. Dara Shikoh, Murad, Shujat and Aurangzeb. As per the 'Will' of Arjumand Banu, Shah Jahan divided her entire private property into two parts one part was handed over to Jahan Ara Begum and the other part equally to four princes.

Unfortunately, after the demise of Shah Jahan, Aurangzeb declared that this division was against the 'Shariat law' and declared the 'Will' illegal and demanded the share from Jahan Ara Begum.

The fact cannot be denied that Aurangzeb, the Mughal Emperor is known as a temple destroyer, fanatic and a fundamentalist.

The historians and the writers have expressed divergent views about Aurangzeb but in brief we have mentioned both sides of the picture.

Wives:—Dilras Banu Begum- she was the chief, Nawab Bai, Udaypuri Mahal, Aurangabadi Mahal, Maseeh-Unisa Begum.

Aurangzeb died in the year 1118 AH (1707 A.D.) and was burried as per his 'Will' and the place was named Khuldabad near Aurangabad.

THE LATER KINGS

The invasion of Nadir Shah was not only the cause of the decline of Mughal Empire but one of the causes.

After the demise of Aurangzeb, within 31 years, the flourishing State fell down as a house of cards. There were seven bloody wars fought within a span of 13 years i.e. Bahadur Shah- 2 wars, Jahandar Shah – 3 wars, Farrukh Siyar- 1 war and Mohd. Shah–1.

These wars were fought among the decendants of Aurangzeb for succession in which large number of princes, nobles and soldiers perished.

Another cause was that the later Mughals did not choose the right person. They left the administration in the hands of incompetent persons.

The most important factor was the involvement of Sayyids. They started interfering in the administration. For instance, when Farrukh Siyar had issued a coin, Sayyids felt annoyed. The Sayyids also played intrigues and politics which was another cause of the downfall of the later Mughals, after Aurangzeb.

Later, the British also took advantage of the weaknesses of the later Mughal Emperors and started their selfish policies of domination.

In fact, some of the later Mughals ruled for a short period as they died at the prime age of their life.

All the above factors are responsible for the downfall of the later Mughals. As a result, the Mughal Emperors could not perform and contribute much to the social and cultural aspects during their period.

MOHAMMAD MAUZZAM MULGHABIB SHAH ALAM BAHADUR SHAH –I

'KHULD MANZIL'

He was born in Rajab 1053 AH (September, 1643 A.D.).

After the demise of his elder brother, Sultan Mohammed, the second son of Aurangzeb, Mohammed Mauzzam became heir apparent. He was suspected for intriguing for power. As a result, Aurangzeb presumed that he was of disloyal nature and placed him under arrest and kept him in prison for seven years. During this period, he behaved with utmost discretion. He was released in 1695 A.D. As per Alamgir's 'Will', he was given twelve subas.

His full titles were Abul-nasr Sayyid Qutub-ud-Din Mohammed Shah Alam Bahadur Shah Badshah.

He was a man of mild temperament. He was learned and dignified. He was a pious person. He visited holy men and tombs of saints. He believed in Astrology. He believed in omens and found consulting astrologers and always complied with their advice. He was kind to his children and their families.

A European traveller who saw him described him as a tall person with a thick beard. He may be considered with his successors as a fairly successful ruler.

His generosity was legendary, but his greatest drawback was his inability to say no to anyone. He was a very successful man of his period. The dignity of the empire was fairly maintained.

He kept his sons in attendance on his person. His policy was successful. His sons did not trouble and revolted against his government.

He had some drawbacks and retained some traces of intolerance of Aurangzeb. There was no Hindu Governor nor any Hindu in high position or independent office. No Hindu was appointed as reporter or *"Waqia-nigar"* and could ride *palki.* When Sikhs were rising, all the Hindus were forced to shave.

Two wives Mihir-Parwar and Amat-ul-Habib survived Bahadur Shah. The second of these ladies was also known as Aziz-un-Nisa Khanam. She was the mother of Rafi-ul-Qadr and had great influence on Bahadur Shah. The other wife was the daughter of Roop Singh Rathor. She was the mother of Daulat-Afza and Mohammed Azim-us-Shan. Azim-us-Shan's son was Farrukh Siyar.

As mentioned earlier Aurangzeb was buried as per his 'Will' and the place was named Khuldabad inAurangabad. Bahadur Shah allotted several villages generating a revenue of Rupees 50,000 a year for feeding the poor and to meet other expenses.

Wives:- Mihr-Parwar or Mihr-un-Nisa Begum, Amat-ul-Habib, Rani Chatter Bai, Nizam Bai, Nur-un-Nisa Begum, Mir-un-Nisa Begum and Zeenat Banu Begum.

There are divergent views about his death. According to one version, he died of cold. The other version is that he was severely wounded in the stomach by his general 'Jensaiati Chan'. The third version is that he was poisoned but no evidence is brought forward.

ABUL MUZZAFFAR MUIN-UD-DIN JALALUDDIN MOHAMMAD FARRUKH SIYAR BADSHAH

'SHAHID-I-MARHUM'

Mohammed Farrukh Siyar, the second son of Azim-ush-Shan was born in Aurangabad on 15th *Rajab* 1095 AH (27th June 1684 A.D.).

Farrukh Siyar married the daughter of Raja Ajit Singh of Jodhpur. She was admitted to the Mohammeden faith. On 25th *Zul-Hijja* 1127 AH (11th December 1715 A.D.), the hena ceremony was performed by applying hena to the bridegroom's hands and feet. The marriage rights were performed by Shariyat Khan, the chief Qazi. The gifts from the bridegroom's side are usually sent a day before wedding which is called the *'Sanchaq',* a Turkey word, they were offered to Emperor's mother and the bride. One Lakh gold coins were offered as her meher. The ceremonies which were observed on this occasion were the combination of Muslim and Hindu customs. The entire *Diwan i Aam* the courtyards, both the roads in the palace and the plain towards Jamuna were illuminated.

Farrukh Siyar came to Delhi Gate of the palace wearing as per the customs the dress sent by the bride of the father. He was seated on the movable throne. The Emperor reached the brides' palace i.e. the house of *Amir-ul-Umra* where women were singing and dancing and fireworks were lit off.

The drinks which were offered to the guest were of rose water, sugar and opium. This was offered to them as per the Rajput customs. Many Muslims drank it and some objected.

There was another thing which was never seen before in the royal wedding. A gold plate was made with five divisions. Every division was filled with precious stones. In one diamonds, in the second rubies, in another emerald, in the fourth topaz and the fifth one which was in the centre of the tray had a large number of valuable pearls.

Farrukh Siyar returned in the night along with the bride to the palace and entered through the Lahore Gate as it is considered inauspicious to go and come from same gate. The Emperor of India observed the customs not to return by the gate by which he went. The celebrations continued till the end of the month.

It is the fact that the most important person in the group of men who came to limelight and among the first rank of Farrukh Siyar's accession was Nizam-ul-Mulk who later established the Asaf Jahi Dynasty. He was a distinguished soldier even in the Aurangzeb reign.

At the time of leaving Delhi, Ajit Singh was appointed to command the vanguard. However, he made an excuse that if he left Delhi, his daughter, the widow of Farrukh Siyar would either be poisoned herself or her reputation would be attacked. Agreeing to his plea, Abdulla Khan handed over the lady to her father. The ceremony of purification was performed in the Hindu fashion and she gave up the Muslim attire. She was sent to her native place Jodhpur with all her property estimated at Rupees 100,00,000. The Muslims felt it undignified specially by the learned and bigotted class. The Qazi issued a ruling that returning a convert was entirely against the Muslim law. Never in the past, a Rajput Princess was restored to her own people after she had once entered the imperial *harem.*

Wives:–Fakrunnisa Begum, daughter of Sadak Khan, Rathore princes daughter of Maharaja Ajeet Singh, whose original Hindu name seems to be Rai Indra Kunwar, another wife was the daughter of Kashtiwar, Gaiti Ara Begum entered the *harem* on 24th *Rajab* 1129 AH (3rd July 1717A.D.).

He died on the 8th *Rabi-us-Sani* 1121 AH (10th June 1709 A.D.). After his demise, he is referred to as *'The Shahid- i-Marhum',* the Martyr received into Mercy.

RAFI-UD-DARJAT MOHAMMAD ABUL BARAKAT BADSHAH

Proclaimed under the style and title of Abul Barakat, Sultan Shamsuddin Mohammad Rafi-ud-Darjat Badshah Ghazi.

Born on *Jamadi-ul-Aker* 7, 1111 AH (29th November1699 A.D.). His mother was Nur-un-Nisa, the daughter of Shaik Baqi. His reign followed that of Farrukh Siyar.

He was the youngest but found to be more intelligent and good in judgement among his three brothers. He was brought for the coronation ceremony wearing ordinary clothes and a pearl necklace. He was seated on the Peacock Throne in the *Diwan-e-Aam* for the celebration of Navroz. He was offered *nazrs* as is usual on the occasion. One notable point about him was that his desent on both sides from Alamgir, his mother was the daughter of Prince Akbar, monarch's fourth son. With such an ancestry, it is strange that he did not display more of the energy and ability characteristics of his earlier generations of his family.

He reigned from his accession on the 9th *Jamad-us-Sani* 1131 AH (28th April 1719 A.D.) to his disposition on his 20th *Rajab* 1131 AH (9th June1719 A.D.) for a period of three months and nine days.

Wives:-The only reference to Rafi-ud-Darjat is the name of one wife, Inayat Banu. He had no issues. The other being Khujasta Sultana Begum.

He died at the young age of twenty years on 20th Rajab 1131 AH (9th June 1719A.D.). Rafi-ud Darjat was buried at the shrine of Khwaja Qutub Uddin.

He ruled for nearly three months. Not many details are available about his administration, social and cultural contribution of that era.

SHAMSUDDIN RAFI-UD-DAULA BADSHAH

Born on 5th *Safar* 1113 AH (11th July 1701 A.D.). He ascended the throne on the 20th *Rajab* 1131 AH (7th june 1719 A.D), in Audience Hall at Delhi in succession to his brother Rafi-ud-Darjat. He was the third son of Bahadur Shah.

It is not known if Rafi-ud Daula was married or not. He was completely under the supervision of Himmat Khan Barha. He was never allowed to attend public prayer on Friday, go to hunting or converse with any noble.

He was very weak and sick like his brother. He was an opium addict, however, on ascending the throne, he gave up this habit.

He must have been 20-22 years of age at the time of his death.

Wives:–It is not known whether married or not. However, his wife's name was given as Sir Hindi Begum. He did not leave any children.

Rafi-ud-Daula reigned for three months and twenty seven days.

The demise of two young emperors during the short spell led to many stories in circulation. Sayyids had resolved to kill the Taihmur's race to enable them to claim the throne. The second version was that since they were addicted to opium which causes incurable diseases. The third version was that they were poisoned.

He ruled for nearly four months, not many details are available about his social and cultural contribution.

ABUL FATEH MOHAMMED SHAH BADSHAH 'FIRDAUS ARAMGAH'

The young emperor married the daughter of his predecessor Farrukh Siyar, her title after marriage was Malika-uz-Zamani. The dower was fixed at Rupees Fifty Lakhs and the marriage was performed on the auspicious day. All Nobles were present. Some of the ceremonies were not publicly performed. Valuable presents were conferred on the emperor's mother - Qudsiya-ul-Alqab Hazrat Begum. All nobles were present. The evening ended with singing and dancing, illumination and fireworks.

He visited the shrines of many saints. He paid visit to the shrine of Panipat. The emperor also visited the shrine of Qutb. He was fond of hunting.

A 'Quran' written in 1247 AD is with Oriental Manuscript Library and Research Institute of Hyderabad-India. This Quran has official seal of two kings. Mohmmed Qutub Shah of Qutub Shahi dynasty and Mughal Emperor Mohammed Shah.

The Jazia or the poll tax has always been felt by Hindu community as an oppression. The Hindu traders seeing the opportunity agreed on a remonstrance against the tax and with one accord shut up their shops. Raja Jai Singh Sawai took up the matter in hand and placed their cause before the emperor. He pointed out that His Majesty was the emperor of the Hind and Hindus were the ancient inhabitants of the country. The men of both religions were equally loyal and it may be said that the Hindus were more so as they depended upon the emperor for protection. When Abdullah Khan's rebellion had broken out, Jai Singh has called on all Hindus to pray for Mohammed Shah's success. Raja Giridhar Bahadur, the Governor of Awadh, added his entreaties reminding the emperor how his uncle Chabela Ram had obtained the same favour from late Farrukh Siyar after his triumph over Jahandar Shah. Yielding to his appeals the emperor abolished the poll tax permanently although it is said to have yielded Rupees four crores of revenue from the entire kingdom.

Wives:–Malika-uz-Zamani, Shah Rukh Banu.

He ruled for nine years six months and one day and died at the age of 47 years.

MOHAMMED MOIZ-UD-DIN JAHANDAR SHAH BADSHAH 'KHULD ARAMGAH'

He was born on the 10th *Ramzan* 1072 AH (29th April 1662 A.D.). His titles were Abul-Fath Mohammed Moiz-ud-Din Jahandar Shah.

He was delighted to see the illumination and the fireworks. He himself used to set fire to Lanka, the mimic fortress of Ravana, the revisher of Sita.

He was the first sovereign of the house of Taimurs who proved to be unfit to rule. According to a popular estimation, he liked liberty of religion.

Wives:- Sayyid-un-Nisa Begum, Anup Bai-She was the mother of Aziz-ud-Din, Lal Kunwar-Imtiyaz Mahal-Concubine, a dancing girl and Shireen Ligua alias Aram Jan.

He died at the age of 52 years. His reign lasted 10 months and 3 days.

His title after death was 'Khuld Aramgah' peaceful in Paradise.

Since he ruled for ten months, there is no noteworthy feature about his tenure.

ABUL NASER AHMED SHAH BADSHAH

The emperor Mohammed Shah had several children born to him, but none of them survived. A destined to grow up was born. This boy became the successor of the Emperor under the title Ahmed Shah.

He was neither a great sovereign nor there is any noteworthy feature about his tenure even though he ruled for about six years.

Wife:–Mubarak Begum.

ABUL MUZZAFAR JALALUDDIN SHAH ALAM 'FIRDAUS MANZIL'

He was known for his weaknesses. One of them was attraction towards beauty, as a result of which he was blinded in 1787 AD.

He was awarded a pension by the British. The amount was less than the Octroi collected from Delhi.

He died on 18th November 1806 AD.

Wife:–Zubdus-un-Nisa Begum.

Eventhough, he ruled for forty years but we could not lay our hands on his contribution to social and cultural activities during his era.

MOHI-UL- MILAT SHAH BADSHAH

No information is available about him. It should be highlighted here that he ruled for one year and a few days.

Wife:–Akhter Banu Begum.

AZIZ-UD-DIN ALAMGIR SANI BADSHAH 'ARSH MANZIL'

He was the second son of Jahandar Shah. Aziz-ud-Din was born in Multan in 1099 AH (1687 AD.). He ascended the throne in the year 1167 AH (1754 AD.) under the title Alamgir II.

His mother was Anup Bai. She was the wife of Jahandar Shah. Anup Bai died in Delhi on 25th *Ziqada* 1147 AH (17th April 1735 AD.).

A minister of Alamgir planned and stabbed him to death. Later, his body was taken and put beside the bank of River Jamuna. A lady saw the dead body and recognised that it was the body of an emperor. She decided to sit beside the body till someone visited. The people started searching for the king and reached the bank of Jamuna. The son of Alamgir, when informed about the incident, decided to make her the sister since she took care of the dead body of his father. She tied a *Rakhi* of the real pearls to the King and the King offered ashrafis (gold coins) and rupees in cash. Akbar Shah and Bahadur Shah continued the tradition.

The lady was Brahmin by caste and her name was Ram Kunwar. She used to go to River Jamuna daily for bath.

Her in-laws were at Mehroli. The King used to visit her in-laws at Mehroli yearly. Bahadur Shah maintained the tradition with the descendant of Ram Kunwar. This ceremony was celebrated by Akbar Shah Sani and Bahadur Shah with pomp and glory.

Wife:–Lal Kunwar alias Zeenat Mahal Begum.

He died on the 8th *Rabi-us-Sani* 1173 AH (28th November 1759 AD.).

MOIN-UD-DIN MOHAMMED AKBAR SHAH SANI 'ARSH ARAMGAH'

He turned out to be a very incompetent person. As a result, the British took away many powers from him, such as, appointment of officials in the Delhi Government etc.

However, he continued the traditions and customs laid down by his ancestors and believed in following them.

Wife:–Kullu Bai alias Taj Mahal Begum.

Akbar Shah Sani died in the year 28th *Jamadi-us-Sani* 1252 AH (9th October 1836 AD.).

ABU ZAFAR SIRAJ-UD-DIN MOHAMMED BAHADUR SHAH BADSHAH

He was the son of Moin-ud-Din Akbar Shah Sani. He was born to Lal Bai (Kullu Bai) on 28th *Shahban* 1190 AH (11th October 1776 AD.) in Delhi.

He had early education in Delhi. Later, he became a famous poet. He was a good calligrapher.

After the demise of his father, his coronation was held as per the old traditions at Red Fort. Bahadur Shah Zafar's coronation was organised in 1837 AD. when he was 62 years old. The *darbar* was also held, a guard of honor was given. After the coronation ceremony, *nazrs* were presented by the princes and the nobles. The *darbar* of Bahadur Shah was an example by itself for the Indians. It was like the *darbar* of French emperors for the Europeans.

Unfortunately, by that time the British had taken most of the control. Though, he was living in the Red Fort but the Englishmen were placed at the gate of Red Fort to guard. He was given a pension of Rupees one lakh. Beside this, he had the income from his *Jagirs.* With this money, he used to pay pension to the poor, Hindus, Muslims and the learned people. A cruel English army officer killed his three sons and his daughter was imprisoned at his residence.

He was a poet of repute and organised poets' gatherings (Mushairas) at Red Fort. The reputed poets of that time were Ghalib, Momin and Zauk. His poems clearly narrate that the person's voice was lost in the lifetime and through ghazals. He used to get mental satisfaction. He wrote poetry in Hindi as well. Besides, Urdu, Panjabi and Hindi, he wrote in Persian as well. He had a different style of writing. One stanza in Panjabi whereas the other in Persian. Similarly, there is one in Hindi, Urdu and Panjabi and vice versa.

During the reign of Bahadur Shah Zafar Red Fort's position was that of earlier period. All celebrations, festivals and literary gathering and mushairas were organised. Here *Navroz* was celebrated, *Shab-e-Barat, Holi* and *Phool Walon Ki Sair* was also celebrated.

A number of religious ceremonies were also celebrated at Red Fort during the reign of Bahadur Shah Zafar which are as under:

Dassehra–Nine days *Ramnavmi* celebration.

Deepawali–was celebrated with pomp and glamour.

Tuladan ceremony was conducted. The king weighed with Gold and Silver which was distributed among the poor. Black blankets, oil and cash were also distributed among the poor. Thereafter, the king takes the bath and change clothes.

Both the communities i.e. the Hindus and the Muslims celebrated each other's festivals and whole heartedly participated in them. Holi was celebrated in Red Fort. All the princes and nobles would participate in it. *Phool Walon Ki Sair* a unique festival of Hindu and Muslim unity and an example of brotherhood was also celebrated at Red Fort.

Bahadur Shah had a great love and affection for his people without any discrimination of caste or creed. He used to help financially to the families of the Hindu nobles and at the death of the nobles, for him, the Hindus and the Muslims were alike.

The people of Delhi were closely associated with the customs of Red Fort. In the eyes of Bahadur Shah, the Hindus, the Muslims, the Shias and the Sunnis were alike. All the communities led a peaceful life. People were happy and prosperous. The Hindus and the Muslims participated in all events, such as, *Rakhi, Phool Walon Ki Sair,* celebrations at Mehroli etc.

The communal harmony of Akbar, and justice of Jahangir are the main features of the Mughal Dynasty. Aurangzeb found to be different from his ancestors.

The British military court issued orders and Bahadur Shah was given life imprisonment and was sent to Rangoon. The broken hearted monarch wrote in one of his letters to his daughter 'The British never lost a chance to humiliate me'.

Wife:–Zeenat Mahal.

He died in 1862 AD. He was buried in Rangoon. He had decided that his crypt should be in the 700 years old shrine of Saint Khwaja Qutubuddin Kaki (Qutub Sahib) and his final resting place should be between Emperor Shah Alam (1759-1809 AD.) and Emperor Akbar II (1806-1837 AD.). But this place remained unutilised.

Among the later Mughal Emperors, he was better. He was considered to be honest, even the British appreciated and considered him to be the best.

If a book is written on social, cultural and religious aspects during the period of Bahadur Shah, substantial material is available.

MIRZA FAKRU VALIHED BAHADUR SHAH BADSHAH

He was the son of the king who got the miniatures of all his ancestors i.e. the 'Mughal Kings and the Queens' made.

Therefore, on his miniature, no mention is made about his date of birth, except the name of his wife, Khanum Zamani nor any material was available on which we could lay our hands.

Wife:-Khanum Zamani Begum.

The Mughal Empire was destined to be ended. The selfish policies of the British were to crush the Mughal Empire socially and economically so that the Kings could never raise their heads and the British could rule India forever.

The British looted India for more than two hundred years and at the time of leaving India, they divided the country into two parts and went back. Thereby, a permanent problem was created.

Chapter – 4

The Queens and The Begums

HAMEEDA BANU BEGUM

She was the wife of Taimur. Beside her, Taimur had three more wives. All the Begums of the *harem* had high respect for Hameeda Banu Begum and love and affection for her.

Hameeda Banu Begum was a scholar and had a good knowledge of Persian, Turkey, Arabic, besides these, she knew Chinese and Zartashti languages.

She was a poetess too and wrote in Turkish and Arabic languages. Her stanzas in poetry were clear and words appropriate.

She used to write letters to Begums of *harem* and to the officials of the State in her own handwriting. These qualities were rarely found.

She wrote two books after the demise of Taimur. One is 'Turki Quawteen' and another is Taimur ki 'Futahhat-e-Hind'.

FAKHR-UN-NISA BEGUM

She went to various cities, such as, Karachi, Hyderabad and reached Lahore and ultimately left for the cities of Afghanistan. It is not clear why and how she reached Taimur. However, from the Persian history, it is proved beyond doubt that she entered Taimur's Palace and within few days she was considered to be among the Taimur's most beloved wife. She was a pious lady. She treated her sub-ordinates with utmost care and distributed money to the poor.

She was the mother of Miran Shah who ascended the throne after the demise of Taimur.

ARJANI OR AZMAT-UN-NISA BEGUM

She was the third wife of Taimur. She was Brahmin by caste. Brahmin army leaders were arrested and were presented in the *darbar* of Taimur and she was among them. She was educated in the school of Brahmins. She was highly educated in Sanskrit. She was taken in the royal *harem*. She was awarded the title of Azmat-un-Nisa Begum. She had three children.

KHANZADA BEGUM

Khanzada Begum was the elder sister of Babar and the aunt of Humayun. She was given the title of 'Padshah Begam' in the year 1532 A.D.

She was considered to be the first lady during the Humayun's time. She played an important role to settle the disputes between Humayun and his brothers. She was the mediator and negotiator between the brothers.

She could succeed in settling political disputes between Humayun and his brothers but she could not succeed in establishing peace among the Mughal family, eventhough she made efforts till the last day of her life.

She died during September 1545 AD. after a serious illness.

GUL BADAN BEGUM

She was the daughter of Babar and the writer and author of 'Humayun Nama'. Though number of authors have written 'Humayun Nama', but 'Humayun Nama' written by Gul Badan Begum is considered to be most authentic. Gul Badan Begum was very beautiful. She was fond of literature and propagated it. She was a poetess.

Gul Badan Begum was born in 929 AH (1523 AD.). According to her at the time of Babar's demise she was only eight years old.

She was brought up in the *harem* of palace by Maham Begum, the fourth wife of Babar and the mother of Humayun. Gul Badan Begum has narrated in detail of this incident.

In 952 AH (1545 AD.), she was married to Khizer Khaja Khan who was connected to the Turkey's Royal Family.

She was the mediator for the settlement of disputes between Humayun and Hindal who was her brother.

When Akbar wanted the 'Tariq-e-Ulfi' to be written in 980 AH (1572 AD.), he requested Gul Badan Begum to help in this difficult task and after some reluctance, she agreed. She was also responsible to make peace between Akbar and Jahangir.

She helped the poor and the orphan. Every year she would organise marriage of two orphan girls at her own expenses. She helped the persons to perform Haj and provided the necessary items.

It is clear from 'Humayun Nama' that besides reading and writing, the ladies at that time were fond of horse riding and used to wear gents clothes. Women were also fond of hunting. At that time, ladies had the liberty in matters related to their marriages. When Humayun wanted to marry Hameeda Begum, she completely refused. Later, she agreed to marry on the advice of her mother.

BAKT-UN-NISA BEGUM

She was the daughter of Humayun and the sister of Akbar. She was famous not only in India but in Asia as well and also in the western world for her foresightedness. She was a highly cultured and well behaved lady. Humayun was very fond of her. She was a very simple woman and had no pomp and glamorous qualities. She was always in simple dresses and led a simple life though she was the daughter of a king.

SALIMA SULTAN BEGUM

She was the daughter of Gul-Berg-Begum. Salima Sultan Begum was the niece of Humayun and cousin of Akbar.

She was a charming and cultured lady. She was intelligent and literate. Salima Sultan Begum was a poetess. She had her own library for which she collected many valuable books and manuscripts.

She played an important role in many ways. She was respected in the palace.

JODHA BAI

Akbar married Jodha Bai in the year 1562 AD. Jodha Bai was the eldest daughter of Biharimal of Amber.

Jodha Bai played a prominent role in Akbar's Palace. She was fortunate to become the mother of crown Prince Salim. After Jodha Bai's marriage with Akbar, her father was given the highest rank. Her brother Raja Bhagwan Das was given the title of *Amir-ul-Umra.*

Jodha Bai's Mahal was spacious, splendid and luxurious. Jodha Bai made sincere efforts to spread education among the common class.

She was greatly interested in trade and commerce. She was probably the first who took keen interest in trade activities. She had her own ships. There are sufficient proofs of her commercial and trading activities.

NUR JAHAN BEGUM

She was the wife of Jahangir. She was a lady of very good qualities and very few ladies of these qualities were found. No one can deny these facts. She loved Jahangir to the extent that it cannot be described in words but she had a desire to interfere in administration of the State. She started ruling herself at the fag end of Jahangir's rule. She herself took care of Jahangir when he was seriously ill and succeeded in convincing him to reduce the intake of liquor.

She was a lady of taste and chaste. She had a collection of valuable jewels and jewellery. She had a shawl studded with jewels. There was a forehead jewellery of Nur Jahan which had very precious diamonds and had no parallel in the world.

In all respects, Nur Jahan was a lady of taste. Her contribution to literature, architecture, garment designing and gardening is well known.

The important among them is buildings, such as, the Tomb of her father, Etimad-ud-Daula at Agra, Nur Mahal Sarai near Jalandhar, the Tomb of Jahangir, Her Tomb in Lahore etc.

Besides these, Nur Jahan laid gardens and her contribution is immense. She took keen interest in trade and commerce. She built market places and *sarais.*

She wanted to make her son-in-law the king but could not succeed.

HAYAT-UN-NISA BEGUM

She was the second wife of Nuruddin Jahangir. She used to advice Jahangir on many issues and Jahangir was following her advice.

ARAM JAN BEGUM

She was the fifth wife of Nuruddin Jahangir. She was a beautiful woman and also intelligent. Though she had no regular education but would solve any problems amicably.

She was considered to be the best player of chess. On several occasions, she won against Jahangir who himself was a very good chess player.

MUMTAZ MAHAL

She was advising Shah Jahan in his state administrative matters. On the advice of Mumtaz Mahal, Shah Jahan fixed a salary of Rupees 300,000 annually to Nur Jahan and never denied any honour or respect. Mumtaz Mahal was famous for her etiquette and manners. She was a kind-hearted lady. She would listen to the requests of the poor very kind-heartedly. She arranged the marriages of poor girls at her own expenses.

Hundreds of murderers and thousands of criminals were pardoned and released and some of them were restored their original positions at her instance. She was known for her generosity. Her generosity was legendary. She was generous toward thousands of widows and the poor. She was a highly religious lady.

On the occasion of his coronation, Shah Jahan organised a grand celebration. Besides precious unlimited jewellery and silver items, he offered Mumtaz Mahal two lakh *Ashrafis* (gold coins). Mumtaz

Mahal sacrificed and offered these gold coins and jewellery on Shah Jahan and distributed among the poor and the needy.

Shah Jahan used to give his beloved Begum Rupees 16,00,000 per annum, but when Mumtaz Mahal died, she had nothing with her. She spent all her money in charities.

Shah Jahan always believed in Mumtaz Mahal and never suspected her in any matter or issues.

On the occasion of the second annual ceremony of his coronation in 1038 AH (16628 AD.), a grand function was organised. Shah Jahan invited all his soldiers to encourage them and offered them precious items as gifts. On this occasion, he offered Mumtaz Mahal Rupees 50,00,000 which was distributed in the same function.

Mumtaz Mahal passed away when Goharara Begum, the fourteenth child was born. Out of these fourteen, seven died at the early age.

Shah Jahan got a golden chandeliar made which was hanging above the cenotaph of Mumtaz Mahal at Taj Mahal. The chandelier had been taken away by the Jats during the occupation of Agra in the seventeenth century. Lord Curzon got a lamp of bronze inlaid throughout in silver and gold which was presented in the year 1905 AD. to the Taj Mahal authorities.

AKBARABADI or AZAIZ-UN-NISA BEGUM

She was the second wife of Shah Jahan. She was very beautiful, intelligent and efficient among all the ladies of the palace. She was most kind-hearted and courteous.

She was very kind to Mumtaz Mahal. Whenever, there was a misunderstanding between Shah Jahan and Mumtaz Mahal, she was to mediate and resolved differences. These two outstanding ladies had a lot of attachment and understanding with each other. After the demise of Mumtaz Mahal, her children had the same respect for Azaiz-un-Nisa Begum which they had for Mumtaz Mahal. Azaiz-un-Nisa Begum had no surviving children.

She lived for twelve years after the demise of Shah Jahan and spent her life in the service of God.

She constructed a beautiful Masjid in Delhi which is famous as Akbarabadi Masjid. It was built with red marble which has an excellent carving work. It has a travellers bungalow and houses around it for the students.

She passed away in the year 1088 AH (1677 AD.).

JAHAN ARA BEGUM

She was the beloved daughter of Shah Jahan and the daughter of Arjumand Banu Begum. She was born in 1023 AH (1614 AD.).

Special attention was paid for her education. She was good at Persian and Arabic languages. Besides this, she had a little knowledge of Turkish language. She was very much interested in poetry. She was a poetess and wrote in Persian. She wrote articles in Arabic language as well.

She was a very good host and a well-behaved and well-mannered lady. There was no parallel to her decency and mannerism. She was fond of simplicity and she always used to wear simple costumes or dresses.

Jahan Ara Begum was once weighed with pure gold and the gold was distributed among the poor. Hence, a weighing ceremony or *Tuladan* was performed. As mentioned above, she was a beautiful lady and was famous not only in Asia but also in Western Europe for her high values. She was also very dear to Shah Jahan. She was a good advisor. Shah Jahan always valued her advice. Whenever, she had adviced, it was difficult to go against it.

She did not restrict herself to the construction of mosques but also constructed *sarai,* palaces, monastry, market place and laid gardens.

She also built a mosque in Agra known as Jani Mosque. She had an artistic sense. Mosques and *sarais* built by her were destroyed during the Mutiny of 1857 AD. She constructed quite a few edifices connected to religion.

She spent her life with dignity and honour even after the demise of her father she gained name and fame.

She died in the year 1092 AH (1681 AD.). She selected her own burial ground in her life time near Nizam-ud-Din Aulia's Mazar in Delhi. A marble *mazar* was constructed. It was beautiful in all aspects.

She paid Rupees 300,00,000 to purchase the land from khadim and mujawar in her life time.

But after her death, Alamgir took Rupees 200,00,000 from khadims on the plea that as per the *shariat,* more than one-third amount cannot be released.

BACHMANI BEGUM

She was the daughter of Shuja and the grand daughter of Shah Jahan. She was very fond of gardening. She was a very calm lady. At her young age, her father passed away. She was shocked at the demise of her father but Aurangzeb told her that he would take care of her more than his own sons. He also told her that she would be treated in the manner the parents treat their children.

It is not known when she got married and with whom. Her date of death is also not available.

SURAIYA BANU BEGUM

She was the daughter of Shah Jahan who was born to Aziz-un-Nissa Begum alias Akbarabadi Begum. Initially, as per the customs of the royal palace, she was taught Quran Majeed.

Shah Jahan had three more daughters i.e. Jahan Ara Begum, Gaiti Ara Begum and Anjuman Ara Begum. They were born to his second wife Arjumand Banu Begum alais Mumtaz Mahal.

On 7th *Jamadi-ul-Awal* 1073 AH (1627 AD.), Shah Jahan's coronation ceremony was held. On this occasion, a grand Darbar was organised. Shah Jahan gave two lakh gold coins (Ashrafis) to Mumtaz Mahal, Rupees 50,000 to Suraiya Begum and Rupees 25000 each to Jahan Ara Begum and Roshan Ara Begum, Dara Shikoh,

Shuja and Aurangzeb were given cash awards as per their positions and status.

Turning to Suraiya Banu Begum, Shah Jahan said, my dear, I know you are generous and if this amount is not sufficient I should be informed. Arjumand Banu Begum was unhappy and said all children be treated equal. On hearing this, Shah Jahan requested Arjumand Banu Begum not to advise him in these matters, in future.

QUDSIA PERHAIZ BANU BEGUM

She was the daughter of Shah Jahan and sister of Aurangzeb. She was a Islamic scholar. There was no parallel to her in Islamic studies. Shah Jahan had a lot of respect for her Islamic knowledge and foresightedness. Shah Jahan also loved her for her personal administrative capabilities and intellectual qualities. Aurangzeb also had a lot of respect for her among all his brothers and sisters.

On his coronation, Aurangzeb gave her 5000 gold coins which she distributed among the poor.

ASAYASH BANU BEGUM

She was the grand daughter of Shah Jahan. She was fluent in Persian and Arabic languages. A highly qualified lady appointed as a teacher under the supervision of Shah Jahan. She was a loving girl of *harem* of the palace. All Begums loved her as if she was their own daughter. Even Aurangzeb used to love her *niece* as she was the daughter of Murad. She was married in the year 1083 AH (1672 AD.) to Mohammed Salah. Mohammed Salah was given an Arabi horse with jewellery, one elephant with jewellery, a *jagir* and *mansab*. Her husband was very fond of her but unfortunately she did not live long after the marriage. She died within six years of marriage during her prime age of life in the year 1089 AH (1678 AD.).

AURANGABADI BEGUM

She was the fourth wife of Aurangzeb. Aurangzeb loved her more than other Begums. A girl was born to Aurangabadi Begum whose name was Meher-un-Nisa Begum. She was born in the year 1072AH (1661 AD.).

She constructed a beautiful *masjid* at Katra. Katra was a business centre where businessmen from different cities used to visit for business purposes. Large number of Muslims offer prayers at this *masjid.*

ZEB-UN-NISA BEGUM

She was the eldest daughter of Aurangzeb. Her mother was Dilras Banu Begam.

She was a beautiful and educated lady. She was a courteous and religious lady.

She had an excellent knowledge of Holy Quran. As a result, she was invited to settle religious disputes at the court. Aurangzeb was very much fond of her.

She was very much interested in literature and spent most of her time for it. Zeb-un-Nisa Begum gained proficiency in Persian and Arabic languages.

She had a library of her own which consisted of valuable books and manuscripts. She also employed many calligraphers to copy rare books. The fact cannot be ignored that she patronised poets and scholars of her time. She spent lakhs of rupees in encouraging education of the poor and the needy.

She was a poetess of repute. She wrote in Arabic. She organised mushairas (poets' gathering). The verses of Zeb-un-Nisa Begum were of very high standard and some of them are found in *Diwan* of Dara Shikoh. After a few years of her death, her poetic writings were collected and a *Diwan* was published. She had expressed in her verses about beauty. Her liberal ideas of religion and religious harmony, pain and misery, she had undergone.

She built and laid a number of gardens including the one at Lahore.

ZEENAT-UN-NISA BEGUM

She was the second daughter of Aurangzeb. The other daughters were Zeb-un-Nissa Begam, Badr-un-Nisa Begum, Zuhdat-un-Nisa Begum and Mihr-un-Nisa Begum.

Zeenat-un-Nisa Begum was born to Aurangabadi Begum on 1st Shaban 1053 AH (16th October 1643 AD.). Her mother was the daughter of Shah Nawaz Khan.

She took keen interest in her brothers. Azam Shah and Bahadur Shah who conferred on her the title of 'Padshah Begum' and doubled her allowance after the demise of Azam Shah.

Lal Kunwar was the cause of estrangement between Emperor Jahandar Shah and his aunt Zeenat-un-Nisa Begum. She was also a poetess which was her hobby. She was famous for giving charity like other Mughal Princesses. She built a mosque known as Zeenat-ul-Masjid at her personal expenses. She said to have built about fourteen carvan *sarais.*

She died at the age of 80 years on 18th May 1721 AD. and was buried at Zeenat-ul-Masjid.

BADSHAH BEGUM

She was the beloved daughter of Alamgir. She was the sister of Mohammed Shah Alam. She was born to Dairas Banu Begum. Aurangzeb was very particular and ensured that his children are taught religion specially 'Quran'.

Badshah Banu, in a short period learned reading and writing. Aurangzeb was delighted with her achievement and paid substantial amount to the teacher. Badshah Banu started writing poetry.

She possessed fair complexion and dark blue eyes. She had a delicate nose. In short, she was a beautiful lady. She led a simple life. This was the only reason Alamgir preferred her to other children. She was a generous lady. She offered lakhs of rupees to the needy. Among all the children, she was the dearest to Aurangzeb.

She was shocked at the sad demise of Aurangzeb and distributed a large sum of money among the poor.

BADR-UN-NISA BEGUM

She was the fifth daughter of Alamgir. She was born in 1057 AH (1647 AD.) to Nawab Bai Begum. Since the beginning, she was an intelligent girl. She was taught Arabic, besides this language, she was taught Mathematics and other subjects. When she gained mastery in reading the Quran, Aurangzeb organised a big function. The entire army was invited on behalf of the government. The ministers and nobles were awarded presents and robes of honour.

It is unfortunate that she passed away at an early age of 23.

AMAT-UL-HABIB

This dignified lady was the wife of Mohammed Shah Alam. She was a talented lady. It is difficult to find an example of her caliber. She always co-operated with her husband.

She always kept her servants happy. She would pay them thousands of rupees in cash and allotted *jagirs.* The entire members and the staff of Shah Alam Government was very happy with her.

She was talented to the extent that her example cannot be found in Asian countries. Many historians praised her qualities and abilities.

MIHR PARWAR

She was the second wife of Shah Alam. She was a beautiful lady known for charity. She was intelligent and a woman of guts. She was eloquent in narration. She was a cultured and dignified lady.

Two wives Mihr Parwar and Amat-ul-Habib survived Bahadur Shah. Mihr Parwar accompanied his body from Lahore to Delhi. The second of these ladies, also called Aziz-un-Nisa Begum, died in Delhi. Mihr Parwar, also known as Mihr-un-Nisa died in Delhi on 11th January 1744 AD. at the age of over 80 years.

LAL KUNWAR-IMTIYAZ MAHAL-ZEENAT MAHAL

She was a dancing girl and made Imtiyaz Mahal after the accession of Jahandar Shah. She was assigned the mansion of Dara Shikoh in the city of Lahore.

Azz-ud-Din son of Jahandar Shah showed his dislike toward Lal Kunwar. Azz-ud-Din was far from friendly to his fathers favorite Lal Kunwar.

ARHAM BAI OR KHUDSIA BEGUM

She was the wife of Mohammed Shah, She was a very intelligent lady.

After the death of her husband during the reign of Ahmed Shah, she made a beautiful garden in the year 1164 AH (1750 AD.) and named it after her. The garden was named as Khudsia garden. It had a *baradari* and a beautiful masjid of marble on which thousands of rupees were spent. The garden was on the right side of the famous Kashmiri Gate in Delhi. During the olden days, it was an example of its kind. The garden had a water canal.

She was an Urdu poetess and her nom-de-plume was 'Ranai'.

AAYI BEGUM

She was the sister of Nijabat Khan alais Sirbuland Khan who was the outstanding general who won the heart of Aurangzeb by his outstanding performance in various wars.

Aurangzeb considered Aayi Begum as his own beloved daughter. She was invited in every function and celebration in the palace.

Not many details are available about her in history. However, she passed away in 1088 AH (1677 AD.). Aurangzeb was saddened on her demise.

Thus, the Queens and the Begums played an important role in the development and contributed considerably in socio-cultural system of that era. Eventhough they lived in the then prevailing social conditions with many constraints. Taking this aspect into consideration their contribution can be considered a great achievement.

It can be concluded that Queens and the Begums were learned, talented, artistic, courageous and above all, they were philanthropic. They were women of taste. Their generosity was legendary.

Chapter – 5

Conclusion

While studying the lives, activities, achievements and contributions in the socio-cultural field we have tried to incorporate the contributions of the Mughal Emperors from the time of Taimur to Bahadur Shah Zafar. Thus, covering the socio-cultural contribution of twenty four Mughal Emperors.

The people were generally prosperous and happy during the reign of most of the Mughals.

It is a fact that the Mughal Emperors contributed in different fields, such as, education, construction of world famous monuments, Hindu-Muslim unity, introduction of culture which is commonly known as the Mughlai culture.

No doubt, Mughal Emperors were ambitious and powerful in many aspects. Some of them were liberal in their approach and others were staunch Muslims. They married Hindu ladies from the Hindu royal families and gave them freedom to follow their religion. However, Aurangzeb destroyed and damaged many temples throughout India.

The Mughal Emperors loved their daughters and made best possible arrangements to educate them. They also helped the poor in educating them. They opened several schools and made best possible arrangements for the education of poor.

It is a known fact that Mughal Emperors not only celebrated Muslim festivals but also celebrated Hindu festivals, such as, *Dassehra, Diwali, Holi, Rakhi, Phool Walon Ki Sair* etc.

Most of the Mughal Emperors organised the *Tuladan* (weighing ceremony) on different occasions specially *Nauroz* festival for themselves and their daughters.

Later Mughals did not choose the right persons. They left the administrations in the hands of incompetent persons, resulting in the downfall of the Mughal Empire.

The fact cannot be ignored that the life of the Mughal lady revolved round the Emperor. The Queens and the Begums usually maintained cordial relations among themselves. The Mughal Emperors not only had Muslim wives but married Hindu woman.

The Queens and the Begums led a happy married life in the palaces. They lived a luxurious life in the palace which provided them accommodation by the Emperors inside the fort. The palaces of the Queens and the Begums were luxuriously furnished and also had gardens, orchards etc. The Queens and the Begums used to wear excellent garments and exquisite ornaments. They decorated themselves not only with the garments made from finest silk and brocades but also ornaments on the different parts of the body.

They were educated but their interest did not end with learning and receiving good education. Many of them were poetesses and composed excellent verses and some of them not only left their '*Diwan*' but collected valuable and rare manuscripts and had their own libraries. They took pleasure in spending their personal allowances for the spread of education, establishing educational institutions and schools for the poor. Some of the Queens and the Begums took keen interest in painting, cooking, music etc. They also participated in political matters and exhibited courage, strength and determination.

They took economic ventures and involved themselves in Trade and Commerce. No doubt they had the backing of the Mughal Emperors.

They constructed a number of *masjids, sarais* and made gardens for the utility of the public. Some of them even selected their own burial place during their life time.

References

PRIMARY SOURCE

MINIATURE

Salar Jung Museum-Hyderabad, India twenty four photo copies of the miniatures of the Mughal Kings and Queens with brief details.

SECONDARY SOURCES

URDU BOOKS

Ahmeduddin, *Mohiuddin Aurangzeb, Abul Muzzafar Alamgir Badshah Gazi,* Publisher Mustafai, Lahore-1894.

Ahmeduddin Munshi, *Jalaluddin Mohammad Akbar,* Anarkali, Lahore.

Assabi Mohammad Intayzam-ullah, *Sawan-e-Umri-Malika Mumtaz Mahal aur Shah Jahan.* Publisher-Murtuzai Press 1255 AH.

Assabi Mohammed Intezamullah, *Bazme Shahjahni,* Murtuzai Press, Agra, 1908.

Baksh Maulvi Mohammad Raheem, *Tazkiray Qauwteen Taimurya,* Quami Press, Delhi, 1902 -1903 A.D.

Baqi, *Humayun Nama, Gul Badan Begum,* Rotary Printing works, Lahore, 1927 A.D.

Hyder Fani Mirza Naseeruddin, *Babar Nama, Translation of Tuzuk-e-Babari,* Translation completed in 1924 under the supervision of Dr Haji Sayed Zeraq Hussain, Mohammedan Printing Press-Delhi.

Khan Mohammad Mashode Hussain, *Nuruddin Jahangir, Refered with Tuzuk-e-Jahangiri,* under the supervision of Sayed Hasan Zahid Jaffary, Hassan Manzil, Shah Gunj, Agra.

Khan Mohammad Mashooq Hussain (Alig), *Halat-e-Nuruddin Jahangir,* Shama Press, Shah Gunj, Agra.

Mehuli Shahid, *Bahadur Shah Zafar Ek Mutalaah* (a study), Ghalib Institute, Aiwan-e-Ghalib Marg, New Delhi-2000 A.D.

Saleem M, *Rangilla Tajdar,* Mohd. Nagar, Lahore-Pakistan, 1958 A.D.

Salik Mohammad Aleemuddin, *Humayun Nama, Gul Badan Begum,* Rotary Printing Works-Lahore.

Sharma Mulk Raj, *Hindustan Ahad Mughalai Mein* (Mr Nicholas Monochi, Storia Do Mo Gar), Novelist Agency Lahore.

ENGLISH BOOKS

Irvine William, I.C.S. (Retd.). *The Later Mughals*, Volume-I, 1707-1720 A.D, Calcutta: M.C.Sarkar and Sons, London: Luzac and Co., Published by: S.C.Sarkar, M.C.Sarkar and Sons, 90/2A, Harrison Road, Calcutta.

Irvine Williams, I.C.S. (Retd), *The Later Mughals*, Volume-II, 1719-1739 A.D, Calcutta: M.C.Sarkar and Sons 1932 A.D, Published by: S.C. Sarkar M.C.Sarkar and Sons 90/2A, Harrison Road, Calcutta.

Mukherjee Soma, *Royal Mughal Ladies And their Contribution*, Gyan Publishing House, New Delhi 2013 A.D.

Swamy K.R.N, *Mughals Maharajas and the Mahatma*, Harper Collins, India, 1998 A.D.

JOURNALS

Monthly *Sabras, Idara-e-Adabiyat-e-Urdu, Aiwan-e-Urdu,* Panjagutta, Hyderabad-500 082, 1963 A.D.

Index

K

L

M

N